THE
ZOROASTRIAN
TRADITION

THE
ZOROASTRIAN
TRADITION

An Introduction to the Ancient
Wisdom of Zarathushtra

Farhang Mehr

MAZDA PUBLISHERS, Inc. ◆ Costa Mesa, California ◆ 2003

Mazda Publishers, Inc.
Academic Publishers since 1980
P.O. Box 2603
Costa Mesa, California 92628 U.S.A.
www.mazdapub.com

Library of Congress Cataloging-in-Publication Data

Mehr, Farhang.
The Zoroastrian Tradition: An Introduction to the Ancient Wisdom
of Zarathushtra/ Farhang Mehr.
p. cm.
Includes bibliographical references and index.
ISBN: 1-56859-110-1
(alk. paper)
1. Zoroastrianism. 2. Zoroaster. I. Title.
BL1572.M45 2003
295—dc21
2003044919

To Vartan Gregorian

CONTENTS

Acknowledgments

The first edition of *Zoroastrian Tradition: An Introduction To The Ancient Wisdom of Zarathushtra* published in 1991 by Element Inc., has been out of print for several years. Given the persistent public enthusiasm for a second reprinting, the Center for Ancient Iranian Studies agreed to meet this demand.

The improvements in this edition include the use of footnotes instead of endnotes and addition of an index, both at suggestion of my learned friend, Dr. Parviz Fozooni. He together with his lovely wife Shahin, voluntarily prepared a camera-ready copy for press and complied the index. I offer them my sincere appreciation and gratitude.

The publication of this volume was made possible by a grant from The Firoz Madon Foundation to which goes my heartfelt thanks.

In preparation of this volume I enjoyed the advice, expertise, and care of Dr. A. Kamron Jabbari, president of the Iranica Institute and the founder of Mazda Publishers, Inc., for which I am deeply appreciative.

Farhang Mehr
Boston, Massachusetts

PREFACE

With the growing belief among scholars in the influence of Zoroastrianism on the Abraharnic and Eastern religions, the dearth of literature in English on Zoroastrianism becomes apparent. "Within the Jewish religion," writes Professor James Barr, "the development of such matters as angels, dualism, eschatology, and the resurrection of the body is commonly attributed to the impact of Iranian religion."[1] After liberation from the Babylonian captivity and contact with the Persians, the Jews abandoned their old idea of *Sheol* and adopted Zoroaster's teachings concerning the hereafter.[2] The concept of reward and punishment in the afterlife, borrowed by the Jews from the ancient Persians, later reappeared in the New Testament. The origin of the Messianic belief, so obscure in Jewish sources, is said to have been affected by the Zoroastrian idea of *Saoshyant*. The result of such interactions is a striking similarity between Zoroastrianism and Judeo-Christian eschatology.

The influence of Zoroastrianism on Muslim Mysticism is evident in the writings of the leading Muslim mystic, Sohrevardi.[3] Also, the similitude of the purification rites and prayers

---

[1] James Barr, "The Question of Religious Influence: The Case of Zoroastrianism, Judaism and Christianity," *Journal of the American Academy of Religion*, LIII/2 (June 1985): 201.
[2] R. C. Zaehner, *The Dawn and Twilight of Zoroastrianism* (hereafter *The Dawn*) (London: Weidenfeld and Nicolson, 1961), 58.
[3] Shahab al-Din Sohrevardi, *Hekmat al-Ishraq* (Tehran: Ibn Sina, 1331), 11.

in The Younger Avesta and the Koran is revealing. The theme of light, particularly in Mahayana Buddhism, is a result of Zoroastrianism's impact on that religion. Alluding to Zoroastrianism and its direct and indirect influences on other religions, Professor Mary Boyce writes: "Some of its leading doctrines were adopted by Judaism, Christianity, and Islam, as well as by a host of Gnostic faiths, while in the East it had some influence on the development of Buddhism."[4] Zoroastrian dualism has profoundly impressed many religions and schools of philosophical thought.

Presently a living faith, Zoroastrianism was the official, or the major, religion of the Iranian empire during three dynasties lasting for twelve centuries. Although minuscule today, Zoroastrian communities in Iran, the subcontinent of India, England, and North America take much pride in their religious culture, and faithfully struggle for its preservation in the face of great odds in our turbulent world. Renowned for their integrity, entrepreneurial spirit, and benevolence (qualities that stem from their religious beliefs), the presence of Zoroastrians is much valued in the countries where they live. Their loyalty to their respective national governments and their commitment to modernization and progress have been exemplary.

The current dwindling of the world Zoroastrian population constitutes a serious threat to the survival of the community – a phenomenon related to the low fertility rate, great mobility, and non-admission of outsiders that characterize Zoroastrianism. For Zoroastrians in diaspora, these characteristics, combined with alienation from their traditional culture and the lack of a native religious context in their new hometowns, have created many concerns.

In India, Zoroastrians, recognized as Parsees, have been the architects, founders, and managers of heavy industries, large banking and insurance establishments, sea transportation, and a commercial airline (Air India). The father of Indian nuclear energy was a Parsee. So were the three high military commanders of the army, navy, and air force in that country during the 1970s. To date the only Indian field marshal is a Parsee, and he is the commander who led the Indian forces to victory in the Indo-Pakistan war of 1971. In Pakistan, the main shipping and hotel

---

[4] Mary Boyce, *Zoroastrians: Their Religious Beliefs and Practices* (London: Routledge & Kegan Paul, 1979), 1.

establishments have been initiated and before nationalization were administered by Parsees. Currently Parsees serve as high officials in both Indian and Pakistani administrations. A number of very large charity organizations in the subcontinent of India are instituted, financed, and run by the Parsees.

In Iran, Zoroastrians gained a then relative socio-economic freedom during the last seventy years and since then have contributed significantly to the development of their country in various avenues of life. They have been directly and indirectly involved in the introduction of banking, electric power plants, and communication networks in many Iranian cities. In recent years, in Iran, Zoroastrians ranked among some of the leading town and urban developers, industrialists, professionals, and public administrators. In proportion to the total population, the Zoroastrians of Iran, more than any other religious and ethnic community, have sponsored schools, orphanages, and hospitals open to everyone, irrespective of creed or ethnic origin.

Notwithstanding many sui gencris and prototypal characteristics of Zoroastrians, most Europeans who have written about them have often confined themselves to a discussion of the community's relative wealth, enormous charity, cult of fire, and tower of silence. Occasionally some have emphasized the role of Parsees in the industrialization of India.

Professor Jacques Duchesne-Guillemin observed that the Parsees became "the Jews of India."[5] Professor John R. Hinnels has wondered why they were not persecuted like European Jews. Some scholars have accurately observed that the Parsees flourished under the British, but have erroneously remarked that they suffered after Indian Independence. The implication that the cessation of British support harmed the Parsees is inaccurate; no discrimination has ever been levelled against Parsees by the Indian Government. Parsees suffered from the act of the nationalization of industries because they happened to own proportionately a greater part of private industry at that time.

In their inquiries, most writers have failed to mention that even in the early seventeenth century, before the advent of British colonization, the Parsees of India had distinguished themselves as prominent traders. This achievement was due to their

---

[5] J. Duchesne-Guillemin, *Zoroastrianism: Symbols and Values* (New York: Harper Row, 1966), 2.

pioneering spirit. Mandelslo, a historian-traveller in the eighteenth century, wrote that the Parsees had already been involved in ship and dock building with the East India Company and that afterwards the British were reluctant to buy Indian built vessels. Western writers normally do not mention anything about the Parsees' contribution to the Indian Independence movement, or about the fact that three presidents of the Indian National Congress, during the first twenty years of its struggle against the British, were Parsees. A statue is erected in Bombay in the honour of one of them.

In reference to Iranians at the time when Zoroastrianism was the major religion in Iran, Professor William Jackson writes, "The Iranian, by influence of his creed, was characterized by action, exertion, and practical values of life."[6] Judging by their present achievements, Zoroastrians still possess the same characteristics; they adhere to the same code of morality and are as active, practical, and constructive as were their ancestors three millennia ago. Surprisingly, seldom have Western writers addressed the question of why and how Zoroastrians have emerged so uniquely innovative, industrious, and humanitarian both in the subcontinent of India and in Iran. Seldom, too, have they conducted an inquiry into the interrelationship between Zoroastrian religious beliefs and the shaping of their character. As in the case of other minorities, religious beliefs pervade the cultural, socio-economic, and political behavior of Zoroastrians, wherever they live. An investigation of the moral, social, economic, and political values of Zoroastrianism and their impact on the members of the community provide an insight into the process of translating doctrine into behavior. I hope this book will serve to explain Zoroastrian doctrinal beliefs in their right perspective and to demonstrate that they, more than the conspicuous and sensationalized fire cult and tower of silence, are characteristic of Zoroastrian community.

Further impetus in the preparation of this work was provided by growing interest in the study of Zoroastrianism in the West by both Westerners and immigrant English-speaking Zoroastrians. This book speaks about the perennial tenets of the faith; it is intended to give a concise and comprehensive account of Zoroas-

---

[6] William Jackson, *Zoroaster, The Prophet of Ancient Iran* (New York: The Macmillan Co., 1899), 150.

trian doctrines. Many scholars believe that these doctrines have had more influence on mankind, directly or indirectly, than any other single faith.[7] At times I have found it imperative to offer my own interpretations of these doctrines – interpretations that are congruous with the letter and spirit of the *Gathas* and in accord with the convictions of the adherents to the faith. To put it differently, in this book I have endeavored to present in the framework of Gathic principles, the body of beliefs of modern-day practicing Zoroastrians. I have refrained from discussing Zoroastrian rituals and have thereby avoided addressing certain controversial issues. Controversies confuse rather than enlighten initiates studying a religion.

In this book, *Mazdaism and Zoroastrianism* are used interchangeably—as are *Mazdayasnan* and *Zoroastrians* or *Zartushtis*. In the interest of a clearer understanding of Zoroastrian principles and in order to stimulate the inquisitiveness of readers, at times I have drawn parallels between some Gathic concepts and their counterparts in other religions, without having in mind any value judgement. I trust those comparisons contribute to a better grasp of Zoroastrianism, and I hope this book will prove of interest to Zoroastrians and non-Zoroastrians alike.

Finally, I wish to express my appreciation to all those who have encouraged and assisted me in this undertaking. In particular, I take great pleasure in dedicating this book to my dear friend Dr. Vartan Gregorian, formerly Provost at the University of Pennsylvania and currently President of the New York Public Library. This dedication is a token of my gratitude for his support during my transition into life in the United States, my new, if not permanent, home.

Boston University

---

[7] Boyce, 1.

INTRODUCTION

History

One of the oldest revealed world religions, M*azdaism,* has, in varying degrees, influenced many religions, including Mahayana Buddhism, Manichaeism, Judaism, Christianity, and Islam.[1] It also has left its mark on several schools of philosophical thought; Plato knew of Zoroaster and Pythagoras probably was a student of Zoroastrian philosophy. Traces of Mazdaism are detectable in both Neo-Platonic and Neo-Pythagorian schools.[2]

The names used for the followers of the religion are: Mazdayasni, Zartushti, Beh-Din, and Parsee. *Mazdayasni* means Mazda worshipper. *Mazda* denotes the Sublime Wisdom; it is the

---

[1] Barr, 201-235; George W. Carter, Zoroastrianism and Judaism (New York: AMS Press, 1979 [repr. from the 1918 edition]), 18-19, 27, 34, 37, 39, 52, 77; Zaehner, The Dawn, 57-58; Zabih-allah Safa, Tarikh Adabyat dar Iran, vol. 2 (Tehran: Entesharat Amir Kabir, 1975), 301-305; Hermann Landolt, "Mystique Iranienne: Suhravardi Sheykh Al-Ishraq," in Iranian Civilization and Culture, ed. Charles J. Adams (Montreal: McGill University, Institute of Islamic Studies, 1973), 23-25.

[2] Alcibiades, i, 122; W. S. Fox and R. E. K. Pemberton, "Passages in Greek and Latin Literature relating to Zoroaster and Zoroastrianism [translated into English]," The Journal of the K. R. Cama Oriental Institute (Bombay) 14 (1929): 22, 28, 54, 65, 72.

name for the God of Zoroaster. *Zartushti* means follower of the prophet Zoroaster and *Beh-Din* signifies the Good Religion. *Parsees* are Persians who fled Muslim persecution and found refuge in India in the ninth century A.D.[3]

In the West, the religion is most commonly called *Zoroastrianism*; and *Zoroaster* is the Greek rendering of Zarathushtra. The general tendency in the Christian world is to associate religions with their founders, a tendency not always welcomed by others. For instance, Muslims do not usually like to be called Mohammedans.

In this treatise, Mazdaism ^{and} Zoroastrianism are employed interchangeably; however, for the following reason the use of Mazdaism seems more expedient. The followers of Mazdaism, drawing on Zoroaster's teachings, are known by different denominations in different parts of the world. In Iran they are called *Zartushti* by non-Zoroastrians, and *Beh-Din* among themselves. In India and Pakistan they are distinguished as *Parsees*. In Europe and America they are identified as *Zoroastrians*. In the holy books of the Abrahamic religions, as well as in most Greek and Roman classical writings, they are referred to as *Magis and Majus. Mazdayasnan*, meaning the followers of Mazdaism, therefore, is a neutral and an all-embracing nomenclature that covers everything and forestalls any confusion. Nevertheless, in the interest of accuracy, I have used the nomenclature employed by a text in its original form when I quote a source.

Because of the antiquity of Mazdaism, certain facts have been lost throughout history, and some extraneous ones have been added in the course of time, all of which have led to factual and doctrinal controversies. As the majority of these controversies concern the periphery and not the core of Zoroastrianism, they are not of immediate concern in this book, which is dealing with the perennial precepts of Mazdaism. The case is different when controversy relates to a substantive question such as dualism, in which case the subject will be addressed at length.

Doctrinal controversies stem from varying interpretations of the *Gathas* (the revealed part of the Scriptures), as well as diver-

---

[3] The date of the Parsees' arrival in India is stated differently as some time between the eighth and tenth centuries. The traditional date is 716 A.D.: Rustam B. Paymaster, *Early History of the Parsis in India* (Bombay, 1954), 4.

gences in *The Younger Avesta* (the part added to the original Scripture in later periods). Other religions experience similar predicaments. God's message, revealed to the prophet, is compiled by the prophet's disciples at different times and some parts are added to it by devout followers in subsequent periods. In such a process, divergences and ambiguities are only to be expected. Unriddling the linguistic difficulties – the vocabulary, grammar, and syntax – of the *Gathas* (the revealed part of the *Avesta*), too, has proved an arduous task, as no other text in Gathic language exists. The presence of ellipses, metaphors, allegories, and the extensive use of figurative language intensifies the difficulties. Although comparative studies of languages akin to, and contemporaneous with, the *Gathas* have illuminated many dim corners of Zoroastrian studies and scholarly endeavors of philologists and historians have paved the way toward a better understanding of the religion, numerous unresolved questions remain.

In resolving doctrinal difficulties, the following points should be borne in mind. First, religion does not flourish in a vacuum, and revealed religion is no exception. Religion grows against a background of deep-rooted traditional beliefs and interacts with other religions, cults, and ideologies. Secondly, being revolutionary in nature, revealed religion comes to transform man's mental-spiritual structure and his individual-societal way of life; as such it defies the established religio-political institutions. Thirdly, in the course of time, man in turn manipulates religion to serve his immediate interests. The history of religion is replete with examples of doctrinal misinterpretation, ideological adulteration, and factual misinformation advanced by both oppressors and oppressed in different circumstances to suit their flickering political and economic objectives. The distorted accounts of the Zoroastrian faith by bigoted writers have caused much confusion. Hence an unravelling of the original doctrines of the Mazdaen faith requires, in addition to philological and theological study, a thorough investigation into the prevailing socio-political conditions of the eras in which doctrinal changes were effected. Introduction of Yazatas into the Younger Avesta, substitution of cosmic dualism for ethical dualism, incorporation of physical resurrection into the tradition, ascription of a supernatural personality to the prophet, and other appendixes to the faith, have stemmed from socio-political considerations in different eras, without knowledge of which our understanding of the evolution of Zoroastrian tradition would be incomplete.

To date, the greatest contribution to the study of the religion has been by philologists and historians; the comparative study of the *Gathas* with the *Rig Veda* has elucidated many ambiguous points. The *Rig Veda* dates to at least 1750 B.C. and is assumed to have great affinity with the prevailing beliefs at the time of the revelation of Mazdaism. Yet, comparative studies in philology, folklore, mythology, and other areas have certain limitations. In drawing and in interpreting parallels, assumptions are made, inferences elicited, and generalities formulated. At best these may be accepted as reasonable probabilities, and reasonableness itself is a subjective matter. Historical and philological studies should be followed with socio-political investigation. But investigation into the impact of politics on religion during the time of the Achaemenians, the Parthians, and the Sassanians has been largely neglected. A greater effort on the part of social scientists in this direction is needed.

The main historical assumptions in Zoroastrian studies have been the existence of a common origin for Indo-European languages and a set of common religious and cultural characteristics for Indo-Iranian ethnic groups.[4] Without such assumptions the investigation could not have commenced. With subsequent reconstruction of the language, culture, and religion, the soundness of the initial assumptions has been re-examined. The similarity between the pre-Zoroastrian religious beliefs and those of the *Rig Veda* is a fact that withstands analytical and synthetic tests. It has greatly helped to explain certain doctrinal divergences that have occurred in *The Younger Avesta*. The reappearance in disguise of the pre-Zoroastrian deities in *The Younger Avesta* and the resemblance of ritualistic adorations directed to Yazatas in the *Yashts* with sacrificial hymns offered to gods in the *Rig Veda,* can convincingly be explained as a political intrusion into the religion, most likely at the hands of the Magis, the guardians of the pre-Zoroastrian Indo-Iranian beliefs. After a period of setbacks in the early Achaemenian period, the Magis managed to reinstate themselves in high religious positions, this time in the Zoroastrian clerical class. An investigation into the time of the

---

[4] Richard N. Frye, *The Heritage of Persia* (Cleveland: The World Publishing Co., 1963), 2 15-25.

restoration of the Magis into the new religious hierarchy will reveal the magnitude of the impact of the politics of the time on post-Darius Zoroastrianism.

Religious militancy is not a new phenomenon. As a socio-political protest movement, it has existed since the dawn of history; its intensity and methods of operation, however, have changed. During the time of the Sassanians, while the incumbent government claimed religious orthodoxy for its legitimacy, political dissidents like the Manichaeians and the militant Mazda-kits were challenging that claim. The rise of Gaumata the Magi during the time of the Achaemenians provides another example of religio-political conspiracy. The religious changes that subsequently were introduced by converted Magis and tolerated by the orthodox Zoroastrianism further exemplifies the influence of politics on religion in that era.

Little is known about the socio-political conditions of the communities in eastern Iran where Zoroastrianism thrived. People of eastern Iran have been sublimely indifferent to history and chronology. They did not establish any system of chronological notation computed from a given date as a basis. Consequently the rapidity with which Mazdaism did spread cannot be ascertained. Mazdaism had to wait a long time for its adoption by the Persians of western Iran and the establishment of the Achaemenian Empire, before entering recorded history. By that time, Mazdaism had engulfed the whole Iranian nation. It is a historical fact that Zoroastrians did not practice forced conversion and, therefore, the multitude of converts must have accepted the faith voluntarily and through conviction. The pull of the new religion came from its doctrines, which answered the individual's spiritual and social needs. The new religion appealed to the populace and the elite alike; its doctrines were holy, straight, humane, practical, and rational. With these characteristics, Mazdaism conceivably must have already been an old and established religion before it was placed in recorded history.[5] The two most controversial issues in Mazdaen history are the exact date and birthplace of the religion. Disagreement is due to contradictory evidence, not the lack thereof. The consensus is that Zoroaster predated the founding of the Achaemenian Empire in the sixth century B.C., and the weight of evidence locates his hometown

---

[5] Ibid., 34 et seq.

in Transoxiana in central Asia. Modern scholars have placed Zoroaster's time as approximately 1750 B.C.

The absence in the *Gathas* of the prophet's personal particulars genealogy, birthdate, birthplace, and immediate family – is not, in my view accidental. Notwithstanding assertions to the contrary by certain scholars, the *Gathas* themselves, if not *The Younger Avesta*, are against cult worship, be it related to the natural elements or to personality. Except for the account of his appointment to prophethood, nothing about Zoroaster's life story appears in the *Gathas*. Without recorded history and without a genealogical list, Zoroaster's chronology remains debatable. In addressing itself only to the religious doctrines and philosophy of the faith and not to the historical facts per se, this book does not enter the discussion of chronology except in a cursory manner.

The extensive political vicissitudes to which Mazdayasnans have been exposed have brought them heavy losses, including that of the major portion of their religious literature. The extant fragments are very small and yet testify to a great religion and a profound philosophy.

The size of the original *Avesta* – the name for Zoroastrian holy books – is uncertain. Two Muslim historians of the twelfth and thirteenth centuries, Tabari and Mas'udi, stated that the whole *Avesta* was written on 12,000 cowhides that were deposited in the treasuries of Dizh-e Nipisht in Persepolis and Ganj-e Shapigan in the Azar Goshasp fire temple. The copy in Persepolis was burned during the invasion of Alexander and the second copy was taken to Athens where it was rendered into Greek.[6] After the eviction of the Greeks by the Parthians in 250 B.C., Zoroastrianism experienced a revival. Although they were Mithraists, a number of the Parthian kings were inclined favorably to Zoroastrianism and one of them, King Volgeses, ordered the scattered fragments of the *Avesta* to be collected. This task was completed by Tansar, the high priest of Ardeshir, the founder of the Sassanian dynasty, who came to the throne in the year 224 A.D. Tradition says that the *Avesta* consisted of twenty-one

---

[6] Maneckji N. Dhalla, History of Zoroastrianism (hereafter History) (New York: Oxford University Press, 1938 [repr. Bombay: K. R. Cama Oriental Institute, 1963, 3; Dinkard, Books 7-9 [trans. E. W. West], in Sacred Books of the East vol. 9 (Oxford: Clarendon Press, 1897), 577.

nasks, or volumes; it was reorganized by Tansar into three parts: *Gassanik* (Gathic or devotional hymns), *Hadha Mansarik* (a combination of spiritual and temporal teachings), and *Datik* (law).[7]

The *Avesta* that has reached us consists of five parts: *Yasna*, *Vispred*, *Yasht*, *Vendidad*, and *Khordeh Avesta*. The *Gathas* are now incorporated in the *Yasna*. *Gathas* means divine hymns. Assertions are made, though not substantiated, that the main part of the *Gathas* has survived. The *Gathas* proper occupy chapters 28-34 and 43-53 of the book of *Yasna*. Chapters 35-42 of the book of *Yasna* form the *Gatbas Haptanhaiti*, or the *Gathas* of the Seven Chapters. Unlike the *Gathas* proper, the *Gathas* of the Seven Chapters were not composed by the prophet but by his disciples. The language is archaic enough to indicate that it was composed soon after the *Gathas* proper, and its implications are divergent enough to show that it was written after the prophet's death. Chronologically, it comes immediately after the *Gathas* proper. Unlike the *Gathas* proper, the *Gathas* of the Seven Chapters are in prose.

The rest of the *Avesta* is called *The Younger Avesta*. Its literary dialects differ considerably from both the *Gathas* and the *Gathas Haptanhaiti*, which indicates that they were compiled long after the prophet's lifetime. The difference in style of different components of *The Younger Avesta* likewise reveals that they were composed at different times. The fact that the language of *The Younger Avesta* belongs to eastern Iran, however, does not mean they were written in that region. Mazdayasnans, wherever they dwelt, recited the *Manthras*, the sacred words of the *Avesta*, in their original language. The priests of western Iran were conversant enough with the Avestan language to author them.

As already indicated, a socio-religious event in Mazdaen religion with considerable political implications was the emergence of the Magis as the Mazdaen priests in the post-Darius period. Magi, by which name Zoroastrians are identified in the Greek writings, was apparently a denomination applied to the priestly class by Indians, Persians, and Babylonians alike. During the Medes, the Magis were a powerful priestly class or clan in the northwest of Iran. They were distinguished by sagacity and a penchant for spiritual and scholarly pursuits. By indige-

---

[7] Dhalla, *History*, 4.

nous customs and interaction with Mesopotamians, they had turned highly liturgical. Although himself a Zaotar, a member of the priestly family of eastern Iran, the prophet Zoroaster had little sympathy for the hereditary priestly classes and no use for their excessive rituals. In the *Gathas* he abhorred formalism and sacrificial practices. He criticized Karapans (priests) and Kavis (princes or priest princes) who kept people ignorant and superstitious. Zoroaster rejected the superficiality of external rites and declared that only through self-realization, *haurvatat*, can an individual attain self-purification. Thus Zoroaster's teachings adversely affected the vested interests of the princes and the Magi priests. The Magis must have resented the new faith; they accused the prophet of blasphemy.

Because of their close association with the Medes, the Magis were not politically trusted by the Achaemenians; and because of their oppressive religious practices, they were not respected by the new dynasty. During the reign of Cambyses, the second Achaemenian king, a Magian by the name of Gaumata usurped the throne.[8] His plot was soon detected and he was deposed by Darius. Thereafter the Magis fell into complete disgrace. Herodotus informs us that after the disposition of Gaumata, the bitter public opinion against the Magis was so intense that the anniversary of Gaumata's downfall became a public festivity called Magophobia. On that day, the Magis dared not leave their homes lest they be molested by the public. Thereafter, in an attempt to regain their lost socio-political status, the Magis changed their policy and gradually entered the mainstream of Zoroastrianism. Thanks to their intellectual abilities, they soon managed to find their way up again into the circles of power. The stone inscriptions of post-Darius Achaemenians bear the names of Mithra and Anahita in addition to *Ahura Mazda*, a fact which betrays the influence of the Magis. This development can socio-politically be explained as a concession to the Magis by Darius' successors in a move to bring about reconciliation between the government and the potentially powerful clan of Magis. Once rehabilitated, the Magis soon regained their old position and managed to reincorporate into the new faith, though in a modified form, many of the pre-Zoroastrian beliefs and practices. "It seems that the Magi took a long time to supplant the religious practices of the Per-

---

[8] See Behistun inscription and Professor Frye's comments, 84-90.

sians by their own," writes Dastur Dhalla.[9] In some cases supplantation consisted of substitution, like replacement of the burial system by the exposure of corpses; of injection, like the introduction of the resurrection of the body; of accentuation of certain Indo-Iranian cultural features and beliefs, like the veneration of fire and the sanctification of the natural elements.

Besides the reorientation of Mazdaism, the adamant Magis, in their patriotism, resisted the Hellenization of Iran, and when opportunity arose, sided with the Parthians in their struggle against the Seleucides. During the Arsacids' reign, the Magis enjoyed a respected and influential social position. They gradually appropriated exclusively to themselves Zoroastrian priesthood and athravanship. Despite the absence of any reference in the *Gathas* proper to the priesthood, the insertion of the following passage in the *Yasna* after the prophet's death is significant: "I repent, am sorry and do penance for any sin I may have committed against my superiors, the religious judges or the leaders of *Magians*."[10] *The Younger Avesta* refers to *Athravan*, the fire priest of the Indo-Iranian period. Under the Sassanians, Magis attained the highest priestly positions and were responsible for the authorship of the whole *Vendidad* – a book that strongly advocates the performance of liturgy and external purification.[11]

During the Sassanian period, Mazdaism became the official creed of state and thus was wholly politicized. Reason was replaced by blind faith and compassion by sheer coercion. Intimidation and heresy charges became the order of the day. Such oppressive measures culminated in the destruction of the Sassanian Empire and with it the decline of Mazdaism.

In its long life, Mazdaism has encountered and been affected by many religions and political influences. Externally it has been

---

[9] Dhalla, *History*, 135.

[10] "General confession" said to have been a practice during Sussanians: R. C. Zaehner, *The Teachings of the Magi* (hereafter *The Teachings*) (repr. New York: Oxford University Press, 1978 [first published 1956]), 120-21.

[11] The priests of western Iran, the Magi, influenced by the Semetic culture, were ritualistic; the priests of eastern Iran, Zoatar, remained faithful to their Indo-Iranian tradition and became less ritualistic. "The vendidad, the antidemonic law, may well have been composed in western Iran by the Magi, who seem to have been the priests of the Medes and later of all Western Iran." Frye, 30.

exposed to Judaism, Christianity, Islam, Hinduism, and Buddhism; internally it has interacted with Manichaeism, Zurvanism, Mithraism, Mazdakism, and a handful of other heretical faiths. Aided by political manipulations, those interactions led to an overall degeneration of Zoroastrianism. In the history of the Zoroastrian tradition, three phases are noticeable. First was Gathic Mazdaism, marked by monotheism, pure ethical precepts, moral dualism, and tolerance. It was the religion practiced by the followers of the faith from the time of revelation through the major part of the Achaemenian period. Second was Magian Mazdaism or the Younger Avestan tradition, practiced toward the end of the Achaemenian and Arsacid dynasties. In *The Younger Avesta*, Yazatas (angels), cosmic dualism, physical resurrection, and ritualism took root. Third was politicized or Sassanian Zoroastrianism, characterized by an official theology, dogmatism, formalism, and intolerance. The politicized religion fostered doctrinal diversions and socio-religious militancy that led to the overthrow of the Sassanian dynasty by the Arabs. In this book, doctrinal beliefs of the practicing Zoroastrians, with reference to Gathic Mazdaism, are explained.

Sources

This book is concerned with the doctrinal beliefs of the Zoroastrians; it deals with the perennial features of the faith. The cardinal precepts of the religion are those propounded in the *Gathas*, reflected in *The Younger Avesta*, held through the ages, and presently practiced by modern-day Zoroastrians. In this book we are concerned with Zoroastrianism as a living spirituality and our prime sources are the holy scriptures and the current beliefs of Mazdayasnans.

Although scattered all over the world, the bulk of Zoroastrians still live on the subcontinent of India and in Iran; hence their beliefs represent the current practice. The Zoroastrians in diaspora in the twentieth century are bound to bring about changes in religious practice that may help the revival, or mark the extinction, of the community.

The Zoroastrian holy scriptures are written in Avestan, a language with elaborate grammatical genders and moods spoken in eastern Iran. The immigrants to western Iran opted for a simpler language, Pahlavi; however they continued to say the holy prayers, the *Manthras*, in the Avestan language.

At the time when Mazdaism penetrated western Iran, Media was a tributary to Assyria. In the sixth century B.C., the Medes rose against the Assyrians and subjugated them. Neither the Median royal house nor the priestly clan, the Magis, professed Mazdaism. The Magis were one of the six tribes in the Median Empire.[12]

The establishment of the Achaemenian dynasty, with their kings professing Mazdaism, gave a new momentum to the religion. Even if they used the religion for political advantage, as has been suggested by certain scholars,[13] the Achaemenian kings were supportive of the Mazdaen faith. The stone inscriptions of Darius clearly testify the adoration of *Ahura Mazda*. With the Achaemenian ascendancy, the influence of the Magis waned. Gaumata's conspiracy to reinstate Magis in power was crushed and the denigration of the Magis continued. Some time elapsed before the Magis, by embracing Mazdaism, could re-enter the mainstream of Iranian society. During Alexander's invasion, the Magis posed as the guardians of the Iranian culture against Hellenic incursion. With the ouster of the Seleucides and the establishment of the Arsacids, the Magis saw the prospects for a comeback into the upper stratum of Iranian society. The revival of the Zoroastrian faith fostered a greater urge in the people of western Iran for understanding the meaning of the holy scriptures. A century of Hellenic rule had curtailed the interaction between eastern and western Iran and thus enhanced the lingual difficulty of communication between the people across the country. The need was strongly felt for translation of the Avestan texts into Pahlavi. In a movement, the aim of which must have been similar to that in the Middle Ages in Europe for the translation of the Bible into modern languages, the task of rendering the Avestan text into Pahlavi fell on the learned Magis.

---

[12] Herodotus names the Magis as one of the six Median tribes that were collected into a nation, Book 1, 101.

[13] Frye, seems to support the use of religion by the Achaemenians as a political device, 89. Undoubtedly the Achaemenians were supportive of the faith.

During the time of the Sassanians, the church and the state were united or rather were regarded 'twins'. Ardeshir, the founder of the Sassanian dynasty, who belonged to the priestly class of Athravans, proclaimed Mazdaism the official religion of the state. He commissioned his high priest, Tansar, to pursue the work of collecting scattered Avestan works, and to prepare an officially authorized text of the holy scriptures. At the same time, the translation of the Avesta into Pahlavi continued and commentaries were added to it, which together came to be known as *Zend Avesta*, (*Azainti* in Avestan and *Avestak-u Zand* in Pahlavi).

With the new role played by religion in the socio-political life of the Iranian people, many religious, philosophical, and literary works appeared in the Pahlavi language, often clustering around the official theology. This is a phenomenon we witness today in countries with theocratic or other forms of autocratic governments. The Pahlavi books were written by orthodox Zoroastrians as well as heretics, philosophers as well as politicians, regime supporters as well as dissidents, and oppressors as well as oppressed. Just as in our time, political dissidents complaining of social injustice voiced their opposition in the garb of religion, be it in the form of the scenario of a visit to heaven and hell, in the context of dualism and martyrdom, in relation to the final triumph of the innocent oppressed, in a social fiction, or in a philosophical framework. Mazdak did not stand for a new religion; he claimed that his socialistic views represented true Zoroastrian religion and contended that the established church had distorted the true doctrines. Mazdak provided the popularized Zoroastrianism of his time.

In the seventh century A.D., during the Arab-Islamic invasion of Iran, many libraries were burned and uncounted books destroyed. Having witnessed in our time the destructive dimensions of cultural revolutions in communist China and Islamic Iran, it is not difficult to visualize the magnitude of the ruinous operations conducted by invaders against the Iranian cultural heritage. Apart from plunder and territorial expansion, the Arabs were determined to substitute Islam for Zoroastrianism and the Arabic language for Persian. After the replacement of the Persian with the Arabic alphabet in the tenth century A.D., many Arabic words were incorporated into Persian language and the Islamization of Iran proceeded at a fast speed.

In the ninth century A.D., during the reign of the Abbassid Khalifs, a number of Athravan priests, including Atarfarnbagh and Adarbad Hemed, compiled the extant fragments of the scriptures and committed to writing the rules and commentaries kept in memory. The result of their noble effort is the preservation of a part of the religious and philosophical literature of the Sassanian era—a salvage operation similar to that in China several years after their cultural revolution.

By that time, however, Pahlavi had fallen into disuse and people could no longer understand the religious texts written in Pahlavi. Hence another development took place. Parts of the *Avesta* were translated from Pahlavi into Persian and commentaries were added to them; this ensemble came to be known as *Pazand* (*Paiti Zaini* in the Avestan language). In the meantime additional prayers in Pazand were composed by the priests and incorporated in the *Khordeh Avesta*.

Thus it is clear that all the extant Avestan texts cannot claim as much authenticity as the *Gathas*. The fact that the *Gathas* are embedded in the *Avesta* does not give other parts of the *Avesta* the same credibility. Nor does it render *The Younger Avesa* into theological canons for the interpretation of the *Gathas*. Assertions to the contrary are based on a misconception of Mazdaism. In connection with the authenticity of various parts of the Avestan sources, chronology assumes relevance.

Zoroastrian literature received three irreparable blows: first, in the fourth-century invasion of Alexander; second, in the seventh-century Arab conquest; and third, in the twelfth-century dominance of barbarous Mongols. The last one turned out to be the most devastating. The Mongol kings, who embraced Islam, combined the acquired religious fervor with their innate brutality; they savagely persecuted all non-Muslims, including Zoroastrians. As a result of these misfortunes, during the last thirteen centuries not only did the number of Zoroastrians greatly dwindle, but over three-fourths of the religious literature of the Sassanian era was destroyed.

Each of the existing five Avestan books deals with certain aspects of the religion and related knowledge. *Yasna*, meaning reverence, has seventy-two *haiti* or chapters and embraces the two *Gathas*. *Yasna* deals with the creator, revelation, eternal law, freedom of choice, purpose of life, immortality of soul, law of consequences, and renovation of the world. The *Yashts*, meaning revered, are composed in praise of the *Yazatas*. As it will be explained later in this book, most of the *Yazatas* do not originate in the *Gathas*. The *Vispred*, meaning all festivals, has twenty-four chapters and relates to the six thanksgiving seasonal festivities, the *Gahanbars*. The *Vendidad*, meaning law against demons and false deities, consists mainly of rules of hygiene. The *Khordeh Avesta* is bilingual and contains the daily prayers, part of which are in Persian. They represent the Sassanian and post-Sassanian prayers.

Undoubtedly the *Gathas* are the most sacred and authentic part of the *Avesta*. They represent true Mazdaism–the religion that was professed and practiced from the time of revelation in eastern Iran. It corresponds to the first phase of religious history. It was also the religion of the realm during the early part of the Achaemenian reign. Mazdaism, at that stage, had "liberator" and "moralizer" functions. It was marked with humanitarianism, flexibility, and tolerance and aimed to remove social injustice, superstition, and the stupefaction of people by false clergy and corrupt rulers–the Karapans and Kavis. The Achaemenians used the religion primarily in moral and spiritual contexts. In the post-Achaemenian era the religion was dominated by the converted Magis. This era was the second phase of the Zoroastrian tradition's development. Magian Zoroastrianism was regressive and ritualistic. The Magis reincorporated into the religion some of the pre-Zoroastrian concepts. The rites assumed greater significance than the substance. The major part of *The Younger Avesta* is the mental child of the Magian sages. A notable scholar has gone so far as to suggest that the *Yashts* in *The Younger Avesta* represent "a polytheism which is very similar to that of the great hymn cycle of the earliest Indo-Aryans, the *Rig Veda* – a polytheism against which Zoroaster rebelled."[14] In my view and for the reasons I shall explain in the section on Yazatas, polytheism in the *Yashts* is more apparent than real. The main objection to parts of *The Younger Avesta* is not the incorporation of Yazatas, but the reintroduction of excessive ritualism, particularly those for warding off evil spirits-practices which are flagrantly offensive to the tenets of the *Gathas*.

The last phase in the religious tradition under discussion is Sassanian Mazdaism, which was politically oriented. The regi-

---

[14] Zaehner, *The Teachings* 14; *also see* Dhalla, 125-26.

mentation of spirituality and the endorsement of class discrimination were its characteristics. At the time of the foundation of the Sassanian dynasty, Mazdaism functioned both as "nationalizer" and "liberalizer". Mazdaism was a unifying force in the hands of the government for attaining its political objectives. From the beginning, in his struggle for power, Ardeshir, the founder of the Sassanian dynasty, politicized the religion, thus helping his ascendance to power. Through the "unifying force" of religion, he also succeeded in eliminating the Hellenistic cultural influence, preserving the country's territorial integrity, and mobilizing the people for the revival of the greatness of the Achaemenian Iran. The Sassanians considered themselves legitimate successors to the Achaemenians.

With the concentration of power in the ruling class, corruption spread, oppression increased, and public dissent mounted. Toward the end the socio-economic conditions so deteriorated that the Sassanian kings used religion only as a "legitimizer" for the continuation of the dynasty. In the sixth century, indulgence in luxury, immorality, and decadence in the ruling class, royalty, and clergy (corresponding to the Kavis and the Karapans of the time of the prophet), became so widespread that finally it resulted in the downfall of the dynasty and the subjugation of the religion to Arab invaders. Such a fate is inescapable for a religion that is identified with the politics of a declining regime.

Next to the Avestan sources are the Pahlavi writings. There is no doubt that many Pahlavi books constitute valuable sources for Zoroastrian studies. But should all Pahlavi books be considered authentic documents on Zoroastrian "orthodoxy"? And to what extent can they be relied upon as such?

Pahlavi books may be divided into two groups. First are the Pahlavi versions of Avestan texts – *Pahlavi Yasna, Pahlavi Vispred,* and *Pablari Yasht* – which should be regarded as religious sources as much as their Avestan counterparts are. Second are mixed Avestan and Pahlavi texts, such as *Afrini-Dahman,* as well as purely Pahlavi books. The list of the Pahlavi books is compiled by many authors and can easily be consulted.[15] Due to

---

[15] Martin Haug, *Essays on the Sacred Language, Writings, and Religion of the Parsis,* 2d ed., ed. by E. W. West (Boston: Houghton, Osgood & Company, 1878), 93-115; J. Duchesne-Guillemin, trans. into English by K. M. JamaspAsa, *Religion of Ancient Iran:* Bombay, Tata Press Ltd., 1973, 13-54.

the paucity of the extant material on Mazdaism, some of these books have received more attention than they deserve. A brief glance at the contents of these books shows that they are concerned with matters of philosophy, hygiene, and law, clustering around religion. The contents of the books should not be taken at face value as orthodox Zoroastrian doctrines. As sources, they should be carefully examined, scrutinized, and used discriminately. A brief survey of some of the Pahlavi books will illustrate the point.

The *Dinkard* is the longest extant Pahlavi book. It is an interesting collection of religious, historical, geographical, legal, and medical information and, as such, a hodgepodge of the knowledge of its time. *Matikan-i-Hizar Dadistan* is a treatise on personal law and the judiciary of the Sassanian era based on the verdicts of some jurists. Presumably, legal books *like Matikan* were numerous at that time, none of which has survived. *Shikand Gumani Vijar* is a scholarly book on the philosophy of religion. Rejecting certain doctrines of Jews, Manichaeans, Christians and Islam the book discusses the problem of God and evil in a broad framework of Zoroastrianism and its related offshoots. *Bundahishn* is another book in this category; it deals with the origin and nature of creation as well as eschatology. *Minok-i-Khrad* is basically a book of ethics that also contains some legendary materials. *Shayast-la-Shayast* or *Pahlavi Rivayat* addresses the problems of sin, the handling of corpses, the issue of impurity, and the proper mode of purification. *Arda Viraf Nameh* is a literary and fictitious account of a high priest's visit to heaven and hell, somewhat similar to Dante's *Divine Comedy* but written three centuries earlier. *Bahman Yasht* describes the triumphs and sufferings of Zoroastrians and gives an account of the Muslims' oppressive behavior.

The world's religious history is replete with contradictory interpretations of holy scriptures, often representing the views of different sects, extending from markedly conservative to pointedly radical. In our time, some scholars have gone to the extreme of giving a Marxist interpretation to certain passages in the revealed holy books. If by some accident only these commentaries survived, posterity would think of them as the only true religious presentation of the faith, and that would be disastrous! Regrettably this has happened in Zoroastrianism as a result of indiscriminate acceptance of all Pahlavi books as sources for orthodox faith.

The majority of the Pahlavi texts that have reached us are scholarly and informative, with a rich philosophical flavor. Some of them have also influenced Islamic (*Shia*) philosophical thought in Iran, but they do not represent orthodox Zoroastrianism. Several of these writings present Zurvanit, Manaecheit, and other heretical views. Most of these books were compiled a few centuries after the downfall of Sassanians in an unfavorable environment. The possibility of additions or omissions, because of fear or oblivion, was present, and at the best they reflect the beliefs and opinions of their writers. Thus caution against the indiscriminate acceptance of Pahlavi writings as a source for Mazdaen doctrine is necessary.

The classical writings of the Greeks provide another valuable, though at times dubious, source. They comprise both statements of facts and expressions of opinions. Factual statements relate to the tangible and perceptible in Zoroastrianism and, when accompanied by a comparison with their Greek counterparts, are more reliable. Factual statements should be taken as valid. This is not the case with expressions of opinions relating to the intangibles in Zoroastrianism. They involve the comprehension of certain highly sophisticated religious and metaphysical concepts of Iranian faith. In order to understand those concepts, the Greeks made parallels between them and their own pantheon of gods. These parallels were often incompatible and at times absurd, resulting in what could be termed misinformation. Some excerpts from the writings of Herodotus and Plutarch illustrate that point.

Herodotus, in the fifth century B.C., wrote: "It is not customary amongst Persians to have idols (images of the gods) made and temples built and altars erected; they even consider the use of them a sign of folly. They do not believe that the gods are like men as the Hellens do."[16] In the same book he also states, "lying is regarded by Persians as the most disgraceful thing in the world. Next to it is the incurring of debt, chiefly for the reason that the debtors are compelled to tell lies."[17] All these are factual statements and are accompanied by comparisons. From these statements, we can infer that the Persians worshipped a non-

---

[16] Herodotus, i, 131.
[17] Ibid., 139.

material and divine god, they did not make an image of god, and they did not lie.

In the following quotations from Herodotus, which contain both statements of fact and expressions of opinions, the position is different. "Persians never defile a river with the secretions of their bodies, nor even wash their hands in one; nor will they allow others to do so, as they have a great reverence for rivers."[18] The first part of the statement consists of a set of facts concerning certain acts from which Persians abstained. The second part contains an expression of opinion which does not present the relevant Zoroastrian belief in its proper perspective. It was not the respect for the river, per se, but the pollution of water that concerned the Persians, no matter where the water happened to be. Water, like other elements of nature-air, soil, and fire-should be kept diligently clean. This is a prescribed religious, as well as secular duty. It is not surprising that Zoroastrianism is labeled the first environmentalist religion.[19] In Zoroastrianism, matter and nature are as good as mind and soul. They are not evil and should be preserved and cared for.

Another Zoroastrian concept often misunderstood and misrepresented by Greek historians is that of moral dualism. Nevertheless the concept left its mark on Greek philosophical thought. As early as the sixth century B.C., Theagenes of Rhegium insisted that divine warfare (battle of the gods) in Greek literature is an allegory of moral conflict in man; several other Greek writers have presented the concept as cosmic dualism.

The Greeks could see that the Zoroastrians were not idolators and that they believed in a transcendent personal and (divine) God, as we have seen in Herodotus' testimony. But the Greeks generally failed to understand the purport and implications of the dualist principle. Confusion might have arisen from their obsession to explain the doctrine through Hellenic concepts of deities. For instance, Diogenes of Laerte writes that Eudoxos and Aristotle had stated that in the doctrines of the Magi there were two powers opposed to each other. One represented the good god Zeus, called Oromasdes or *Ahura Mazda*, and the other represented the devil Hades, called Areimandios or Angramainyo. On

---

[18] Ibid.

[19] Homi B. Dhalla, "*The Avestan View of Ecology*," Shiraz: Pahlavi University, 1974.

the same subject, Plutarch writes: "Oromondes sprang out of the light and among all things perceived by the senses that element most resembles it; Areimandios sprang out of darkness and is therefore of the same nature with it."[20] These excerpts reveal that Plutarch had not grasped the Zoroastrian concept of God. Zoroaster, in no unequivocal terms, proclaimed that *Ahura Mazda* created every good thing, including light, and that light emanated from, or was created by, God. Thus God cannot have sprung out of light as Plutarch asserts, but it is light that flows from God. In Mazdaism, God is represented as much by light as by truth and righteousness. Greek writings inform us that the well-known physician to King Artaxcerxes II, Ktesias (B.C.400), the philosophers Theopompos of Chios (B.C.300), and Hermippos of Smyrna (B.C.250), had intellectual intercourse with the Magis.[21]

Other sources for Zoroastrian studies are the works of Christian writers, mainly the Armenians, during the Sassanian era, and the Muslim writings of the post-Sassanian era. For the reasons mentioned below, these writings, too, need special scrutiny before being considered as valid sources for Zoroaster's theology. For the reasons discussed here, many of the writings of the Christian historians of this period seem to contain misinformation, just as the Greek writings did.

Although the war between Rome and Persia began in the first century B.C., it intensified from the third century A.D. onward, until Iran was defeated and subjugated by Arabs in the seventh century A.D. From the third century A.D., the Zoroastrian religion became the official creed of the Persian Empire. Roughly a century later, Constantine proclaimed the Roman Empire as Christian, with himself as the defender of that faith, requiring loyalty from all Christians, irrespective of their citizenship.

During the third and fourth centuries, three matters were of particular concern to the Sassanians. Firstly, the Arsacids, who ruled Iran before the Sassanians, had survived in Armenia and enjoyed the protection of the Romans, and thus constituted a potential political threat to the Sassanians. (The Arsacid king, Vologeses, in the year 62 A.D. put his younger brother Tiridates, who professed Zoroastrianism, on the Armenian throne. Tiridates' successors continued to rule Armenia even after the estab-

---

[20] Haug, 8.
[21] Ibid., 7.

lishment of the Sassanians, and Armenia, which once was a stronghold of Zoroastrianism, in defiance of the Sassanians, turned Christian.) Secondly, Armenians, who had embraced Christianity, displayed loyalty to Rome and posed a potential religious and political menace to the Sassanian Empire. Thirdly, Christian dogmas from without and Manichaean doctrines from within were challenging the official religion of the state. The prolonged war between Iran and Rome, often instigated by the Armenians, had poisoned the minds of contemporaneous historians. Therefore, the historical accounts of that era are mostly biased and politically motivated. The following extracts from the writings of some Christian writers of that period illustrate that point.

Theodoros of Mopsuestia Damascius, the Christian Greek writer who lived during the Sassanian era, called Mazdaism primitive and by ascribing Zurvan's doctrine of creation to Zoroaster tried to falsify the latter's claim to monotheism. The Armenian writer Elisaeus, in his famous history book *Vartan*, written in the fifth century, refutes Zoroastrian beliefs.

Another Armenian historian, Eznic, in his book against heretical opinions, reflects upon Zoroastrianism in a lengthy account in which he presents Zurvan's doctrines of creation as that of Zoroaster. He writes: "Before anything, heaven or earth, or creature of any kind whatever therein was existing, Zurvan existed whose name means fortune or glory."[22] That is why the warning against such writings is repeated in this book. Before relying on them as sources for Zoroastrian doctrines, a thorough evaluation of their credibility is essential. They may, however, be usefully consulted for other information. Both these Armenian writers inform us that in the fifth century A.D. at least two Zoroastrian sects existed that were inimically opposed to each other. One was called Mog (Magi, Maghava), and the other Zendik; the former was mostly influential in western Persia, and the latter in eastern Persia, useful information on schism at that time. A look at the geographical centers of the two sects may help to determine their orthodoxy.

Prejudice and misinformation, similar to that described above, is detectable in the writings of many Muslim historians, some of whom, like Dimishgi (A.D.1327), have gone so far in

---

[22] Ibid., 13-14.

their animosity as to identify the Magi with idolators. Dimishgi lived at a time when the persecution of non-Muslims in Iran, particularly Zoroastrians, was at its height. In contrast, a celebrated and renowned Muslim historian Shahrestani (A.D.1153) states in his famous work, *Kitabu-l-Milal va Nahal* (On Religious Sects and Creeds) that Zoroastrianism, being a revealed religion, comes under the same category as Judaism and Christianity. For him, Zoroastrianism was a religion that believed in monotheism, revelation (via the holy scriptures), and the Day of Judgment. The followers of such religions in Islam are designated Ahl-e Ketab (Believers in the Revealed Books) and are treated as Zimmis. The Zimmis had to pay poll taxes and submit to Islamic rule, in return for which they were allowed to practice their religion. While Christians and Jews were definitely considered Zimmis, the Zimmi status of Zoroastrians, notwithstanding references to Majus in Koran and Hadiths, has been a subject of argument. In an attempt to save Zoroastrians from persecution, some well-wishing Irani Muslims identified Zoroaster with Ibrahim, a claim that lacks historical evidence. In their enthusiasm to save their old heritage, other Iranian Muslims assigned Zoroastrian fire temples and mausoleums to Shi'a Imarns or Ibrahimian prophets. For instance, the tomb of Cyrus the Great in Fars was ascribed to King Solomon's mother and a famous fire temple in Azerbayejan to King Solomon himself.

In post-Mohammedan Iran, despite all the official efforts to eliminate the Iranian religion, Zoroastrianism influenced many Muslim theosophical schools. The most notable is the mystic school of Shahab al-Din Sohrevardi and his Ishraq philosophy in the twelfth century. Sohrevardi, who believed in intuition, personal discovery, God's unveiling, and visionary perception (*Kashf* and *Shohud*) as the means of realization of truth, explicitly admitted that he was following the path trod before him by Frashaoshtra and Jamaspa, both of whom were among the first disciples of Zoroaster. Sohrevardi perceived God as the Light of Lights; the most important radiation of that source was *Bahman* or *Vohu Mana*. Sohrevardi's philosophy was taken up and expounded by great philosophers like Mohamad Shehrzouri and Mulla Sadra.[23] Zoroastrianism also clearly left its mark on the Mu'atazilite school, in which the central idea is the unity and

---

[23] Safa, 301.

justice of God. In this Islamic school, justice is a rational comprehensive concept; God has to act in accordance with justice and thus is not the author of injustice or evil.[24] This is one of the main features of the concept of God and the law of *Asha* in Zoroaster's teachings.

After eleven centuries of silence and abeyance, Zoroastrianism found its way into the European institutes of higher learning in the eighteenth century. This was due to the scholarly genius and indefatigable efforts of several European scholars. In the nineteenth century, inspired by the Zoroastrian dualist concept and the final victory of good, Friedrich Nietzsche ascribed his own philosophy to Zoroaster; and Richard Strauss, impressed by Nictzsche's work, named one of his symphonies after Zoroaster. In the eighteenth century, Zoroastrianism attracted French writers like Voltaire and Diderot. The French writers stood for "natural religion" and were opposed to the monopoly of truth by the Catholic Church. They saw Zoroastrian monotheism as a "weapon" to be used against Christianity, showing that "Moses was not unique: truth could be found in non-Christian tradition, too."[25] The first European scholar responsible for reintroducing Zoroastrianism to the Western world was the Oxford University professor Hyde. His learned work entitled *Historia religionis veterum Persarum eorumque Magorum*, published in 1700, incorporates much information about the Parsees' religion and their belief in monotheism, which particularly attracted Western scholars. Hyde did not know Avestan and Pahlavi, and therefore his knowledge of Zoroastrianism and the religion he presented was based on what he had learned from the Parsees. It was the faith that was being practiced by the Parsees in India, free from scholastic speculation or philological interpretation. Then there came the work of the celebrated French scholar Anquetil du Perron, who in 1711 published the first translation of what he had named *Zend-Avesta*, comprising the theological and moral principles as well as the ceremonies of the divine services. Although numerous inaccuracies were subsequently detected in his translation, his pioneering work has retained its place of distinction. He paved the way for further systematic research in Zoroastri-

---

[24] Ibid., 304.

[25] J. Duchesne-Guillemin, "The Western Response to Zoroaster" (hereafter "The Western Response") from the Ratanbai Katrak Lectures of 1956 (Westport, Conn.: Greenwood Press, 1973), 15.

anism, both in the West and by Parsees in India. Anquetil du Perron had studied *Zend-Avesta* in India against a background of mistrust and suspicion by the Parsees. He had no prior acquaintance with Avestan grammar or philology and had to fight his way against many physical and scholastic odds.

Subsequent to du Perron's translation, many scholars studied Zoroastrianism and their views range from a denial of the prophet to the acknowledgement of one whose religion has influenced virtually all subsequent religions; from absolute monotheism to theological dualism; from a great body of moral teaching to the art of witchcraft; from a sublime philosophy of life to a primitive code of behavior. Given the limitations and prejudices of the human mind and the antiquity of Mazdaism, such divergence of opinion is only to be expected. Controversies continue and will extend into the future and that is what makes the study of Zoroastrianism ever more challenging.

Method of Investigation

Investigation is first made into the beliefs of the practicing Zoroastrians in Iran and the subcontinent of India. Then the tenets of the faith in action are explained within the Gathic doctrinal framework. In this endeavor, philological investigations, theological interpretations, and historical evidences are consulted. The doctrinal changes are examined and explained in the light of socio-political forces operating in each distinct historical era. No scholarly speculation is taken on face value.

Among the various translations of the *Gathas*, I have preferred translations by Dr. Iraj Taraporewala and Dinshah Irani because they, as practicing Zoroastrian scholars, have a better grasp of the spirit of the *Gathas* than non-Zoroastrian scholars.

I consider the reading of conflict between the settled agricultural life and the nomadic life—or the conflict between sown and steppe—into the *Gathas*, as suggested by some scholars, most inaccurate. The use of the following terms in *Avesta*: *nmana* (family), *vis* (unit of settlement, which can be compared to clan, village, or city), *Zantu* (territory) and *khshatra* (people with the same culture, interests, and aspirations, comparable to nation), show that Zoroaster preached for the settled people in a vertically structured society and not only for nomads.

The affinity between Vedic and Gathic languages and the common mythology of the Indo-Iranian people should not be stretched unreasonably into every corner of the Zoroastrian faith. The use of analogies has its limitation. For instance, it has proved helpful in explaining the process of reintroduction into *The Younger Avesta* of the Indo-Iranian deities in the form of the Yazatas.

Our starting point is that Zoroaster preached a new religion. He broke away from the rituals associated with the worship of *daevas*, including the excessive use of *Haoma*, and drew a line between theology, mythology, and epic tradition–a line which is marred in *The Younger Avesta*. He rejected the idea of the divine descent of the rulers on earth and invited people to stand against injustice. The reappearance of the rituals in *The Younger Avesta* and the manipulation of the religion for political aims by princes and priests of the Sassanian period is explained.

Controversial questions, like ethical versus cosmic dualism, are presented without value judgment. The belief of the practicing Zoroastrians on this matter, and the process of the change of the Gathic ethical dualism to the younger Avestan cosmic dualism is described. In relation to monotheism in Zoroastrian tradition, the validity of factual testimonies of writers like Hyde, Mandelslo, and Chevalier de Chardin are examined and weighed against the speculations of scholars like Henning.

The Structure of the Work

As previously mentioned, this book is concerned with the doctrinal beliefs of the practicing Zoroastrians, which will be examined within the framework of the Gathic principles. Variances in the current practice will be considered.

In my view, the *Gathas* promulgated seven new and, at that time, revolutionary concepts which affected man's philosophy of creation and mode of life for millennia to come. These concepts constitute the Zoroastrian doctrines which are still believed and practiced by the followers of the faith. Asked about his or her beliefs, a Zoroastrian enumerates beliefs in the following: *Ahura Mazda* as the one God, Zoroaster as the God's prophet, *Asha* as God's will, existence of the good and evil, the ongoing act of creation, life after death, yield (heaven and hell), and the final triumph of goodness. We discuss and interpret these beliefs within the framework of the Gathic doctrines in seven chapters.

Chapter One: In the first chapter the belief in one God, *Ahura Mazda*, the principle of unity, constructivity, goodness, and justice are discussed. The prophet saw spiritual unity in plurality. He proclaimed that there is one Being (*Ahura*) and that Being is the source of all the others. He further declared that "Being" has no beginning and no end. "Being" has no origin and thus any suggestions about the existence of a primordial state of "non-Being" would be unreasonable. This is theological monotheism. Unlike the Greek philosophers, Zoroaster did not consider the universe as being developed from a basic substance. The source is not a basic substance but a divine Being. Goodness, constructiveness, and justice are central in the concept of *Ahura Mazda*.

Chapter Two: In this chapter the principles of prophethood and revelation are discussed. Zoroaster perceived *Ahura Mazda* through the inner eves of mind and conscience. God does not appear to Zoroaster in the clouds or in fire; nor does the prophet ascend to the sky to see God.

The *Gathas* depict prophethood as a two-way process. The first stage relates to the establishment of a direct relationship with God through theosophic contemplation; the second is revelation of God's message. Zoroaster saw God only in his attributes. Glimpses of those attributes radiate within each human being. This concept is another feature of belief in the unity of Being (short of belief in Pantheism). Zoroaster was the first prophet to introduce God as holy intelligence and wisdom and to see human beings as the possessors of holy intelligence and as coworkers and friends of God. As coworkers, they can develop and enhance their intelligence and use it for the advancement of the world and the prosperity of mankind.

Chapter Three investigates the principle of *Asha*–eternal divine law, order, justice, righteousness, and progress. *Asha* lies at the foundation of Mazdaism. The practicing Zoroastrians call it God's will. A moral, practical, orderly life is the major concern of Zoroaster. For him the struggle between good and bad continues until the time when good irrevocably triumphs. Mazdaism gave purpose, hope, and self-dignity to human beings. The idea of the unity, goodness, and justice of God is in Zoroastrianism; the implication is that God has to act in accordance with justice.

Chapter Four concerns good and evil. The principle of moral dualism is a cardinal tenet of Zoroastrianism. The prophet said that at the beginning of the appearance (or creation) of man, the two mentalities manifested themselves in man's mind, word, and deed. One was good; the other evil. From their encounter life and nonlife came into existence. Thus, according to Zoroaster, while Being has no origin, life and nonlife have. Evil has an origin and cannot be primordial. *Ahura Mazda* designed both *Mainyava and Gaethya*; in both of these worlds, dualism is conceivable, but with *Ahura Mazda* there cannot be dualism. The Platonic Academy, in the fourth century B.C., showed a great interest in Zoroastrian dualism. This principle is discussed in Chapter Four where the concept of evil is explored.

Chapter Five explains the nature of *Spenta Mainyu*, the augmentive and creative spirit. The belief in a creative, augmentive, and developmental force operating in this world (*Spenta Mainyu*) is fundamental to Zoroastrianism. Zoroaster gave great attention to the physical world and the powers operative in the universe. He identified two divine media for the attainment of progress, both of which are attributes of *Ahura Mazda*. The two media are *Asha* (order and justice), discussed in Chapter Three, and *Spenta Mainyu* (the creative, augmentive, and developmental force) explained in this chapter. God does not recreate the world in infinitesimal points of time; nor did he create it once forever. According to the principle of *Spenta Mainyu*, creation is an ongoing process. God is the first cause; secondary causes exist according to the law of *Asha*. In Mazdaism, creation approximates emanation, shaped by God.

Chapter Six presents the law of consequences. The concept of heaven and hell (yield or reward and punishment) was first introduced by Zoroaster. Jews, before coming into contact with Zoroastrians, believed that all individuals, irrespective of their life records in the world, would transform into a shadowy existence, *sheol*, and live in a dark place at the bottom of the earth. In the post-exile period this attitude changed and the idea of reward and punishment appeared in Judaism and later in other revealed religions.

Chapter Seven is devoted to an explanation of the principle of the final triumph of good over evil, or, as it is generally known, the establishment of God's kingdom on earth. Man's struggles will culminate in a complete refreshment (or renovation) of the world. This process, however, is gradual. The promised final victory of goodness pours hope and happiness into the hearts of all who work for the happiness of others. As coworkers of God, man must cooperate with *Spenta Mainyu* in harmony with *Asha*, in order to replace conflict with harmony and misery with happiness. The physical world is given by God and therefore is not evil. Man, as the custodian of nature, must care for nature and the environment and with good deeds establish the kingdom of God on earth.

I

ONE GOD: *AHURA MAZDA*

The Principle of Monotheism

Not only did I conceive of Thee, O Mazda,
As the very First and the Last
As the Most Adorable One,
As the Father of Good Thought,
As the Creator of the Eternal law of Truth and Right,
As the Lord Judge of our actions in Life,
I beheld these with my very eyes.

(Gathas: Yasna 31-8)

Ahura Mazda

He is the Absolute, the All-Perfect, the Spirit of Spirits, the Essence of Being, the First Cause, the Creator, the Sustainer, the Source of Goodness, the Father and essence of Wisdom, the Nature of Truth, the Quintessence of Justice, the Boundless Constructive Power, the Eternal Law, the Unchangeable, the Ultimate Reality, and the Only Adorable One to be worshipped; and thus he is proclaimed and preached by Ashu Zarathushtra.[1]

---

[1] *The Gathas:* Father of Truth: *Yasna* 44-3, 47-2; All Goodness: *Yasnas 44-6 to 15, 33-10,11,12*; First and last: *yasna* 31-8; Sublime and the Greatest of All: *Yasmas 43-5,13 32, 45-6*; Father of Wisdom: *Yasnas* 31-8, 45-4; Father of Love *Yasnas 31-8, 45-8*; Spirit of Spirits: *Yasna* 51-7; Lord of Matter and Life: *Yasnas* 31-11, 28-2; Creator and Sustainer: *Yasnas 31-9, 44-3, 4, 5, 51-7*; Light of Lights: *Yasnas 31-7*; Justice 30-11, 32-8, 15, 33-1.

Ahura Mazda is transcendent, immanent, and a-personal. In his Transcendence, he is infinitely great and beyond all creations.[2] He is independent of the cosmos, but the cosmos depends on him. He has no spatial location. Revelation, prophethood, and intuition relate to the transcendence of God.[3]

In his Immanence, he manifests himself in the entire creation.[4] He is present everywhere in the cosmos: in the grains of sands, in the seeds of the plants, in the being of animals, and in the spirit of man. He is in and with, as well as out and beyond, all creations. He is beyond time and space, though time and space are with and in him. All creations exist in the presence of God. Cosmos does not veil God, nor is it his body; and like creation, cosmos has a soul.[5] It is an expression of God's creativity.[6]

In his a-personality, he is not a person, but has a personal relationship with man. He created man but is not his father. He is abstract yet real; he is a pure monad and devoid of anthropomorphic traits. He is the essence of consciousness without a conscious self.[7] God has no shape or form and does not appear in any material substance. Few references to God's all-seeing eyes and reward-distributing hands should be taken as metaphors and poetic license in the attempt to describe God's infinite attributes by analogy with finite concepts in a language easily understood by ordinary people. Anthropomorphic ideas are rarer in the *Gathas* than in all other holy scriptures.[8] In the Gathic tradition, *Ahura Mazda* is personal in his relationship to man; and in *The Younger Avesta*, as the Godhead, he becomes impersonal.

---

[2] The *Gathas*: Spirit of Spirit and the Essence of Wisdom, Life and Sublime, He is beyond the universe: *Yasnas*: 43-5,6,7,11, 45-6.

[3] The *Gathas:* Divine and Most Holy: *Yasna* 43-5,9, 51-1,7, 29-8.

[4] The *Gathas*: Through *Spenta Mainyu,* the Attributes of God Manifest themselves in this world: *Yasnas* 31-7, 33-5 34-2, 43-2, 43-9,10,11, 47-1, 2, 3, 48-3,4,6.

[5] The *Gathas*: *Yasna* 29-1.

[6] The *Gathas*: God created and fashioned the world *Yasna* 29-1; God created the earth to give man joy, *Yasna*, 47-3.

[7] *Haurvatat* represents Perfection and Consciousness in the case of *Ahura Mazda*; it represents perfection and self-consciousness in the case of man.

[8] Carter, 43.

Ahura Mazda is ineffable and appears to man only in his attributes. According to the *Gathas* he is the Essence and Father of
Intelligence, Righteousness-with-justice, Tranquility-with-Love,
Divine Might, Perfection, and Eternity. He is the Light of Lights,
and all goodness emanates from him. His attributes are ethereal-
ized moral concepts expressed in pure abstractions, although in
The Younger Avesta they are personified as archangels. *Ahura
Mazda* is made into attributes[9] and the glimpses of these attributes dwell within each and every human being. Man, being the
coworker of God, can interact with God if he so chooses. In this
network of relationships, the attributes of God are manifested
and are conceptualized by finite man. It is only through these
attributes that finite man can comprehend and describe the oth-
erwise inexplicable and infinite *Ahura Mazda*. Goodness, constructiveness, and justice are central to Zoroaster's concept of
Ahura Mazda.

The term *Ahura Mazda* signifies the Lord of both celestial
and terrestrial worlds. *Ahura* stems from the root *Ah*, meaning
"to be, to exist," and *Mazda* from *Mana*, meaning wisdom and
intelligence. *Ahura Mazda* is the Essence and Source of Being
and Wisdom.[10] Wisdom and justice are the constant threads running through the entire *Gathas*—the holy scripture of Zoroastrians. The importance of wisdom is also reflected in the *Vohu
Mana*, which is the first mentioned epithet as well as the first
creation of God.

---

[9] Cf. the Gospel according to Saint John (1: 14): "And the word was
made flesh, and dwelt among us, and we viewed His Glory-such glory
as the only-begotten Son received from His father-abounding in Grace
and Truth. Also with Exodus 19:18, 19: "And Mount Sinai was altogether on a smoke because the Lord descended upon it in fire; and the
smoke thereof ascended as the smoke of furnace, and the whole mount
quaked greatly. And when the voice of the trumpet sounded long; and
waxed louder and louder, Moses spake and God answered him by a
voice." In the Old Testament God often appears in the sky, in the cloud,
and in the fire and addresses the people of Israel and the prophet
Moses; in the *Gathas* God always acts through his attributes and addresses people or the prophet Zoroaster often through *Vohu Manah*
(good mind), *Asha* (truth) and *Sraosha* (religious conscience). The
Gathas: Yasna 28-5.

[10] The thread of holy wisdom, good mind, and righteous reasoning runs
through the *Gathas* and is reflected in the most commonly used God's
name, *Mazda*.

The six cardinal epithets of *Ahura Mazda,* which in *The Younger Avesta* came to be known collectively as *Amesha Spenta,* are Sublime Wisdom, Righteousness (justice), Divine Might, Love, Perfection (wholeness), and Immortality. Rather than accidents, they are the quintessence of *Ahura Mazda.* While each of these qualities in its sublimity and universality represents *Ahura Mazda,* none of them is *Ahura Mazda; Ahura Mazda* is each and all of them. Although they are seven, they are one thought, one word and one deed; they are father and children; they are source and rays of light; and they present plurality in oneness.

(1) Sublime Mind, *Vahishta Mana,* is the essence of wisdom and intelligence. It is the universal mind. Good mind is the first creation of *Ahura Mazda.* The *Gathas* state that *Ahura Mazda* conceived the universe in his universal mind, which is the essence of good mind. In the hierarchy of the attributes, good mind comes first. All these indicate the importance of good thought and sound reasoning in Zoroastrianism.

(2) Sublime Righteousness and Justice are the same and are represented by *Asha Vahishta.* Righteousness is justice and justice is righteousness; *Asha Vahishta* is universal justice and Ideal Truth. *Asha Vahishta* also represents the eternal law that governs the universe. It designates both natural and divine laws, which coincide. *Ahura Mazda* is the law-giver and the judge. Asha represents *Ahura Mazda*'s will. It stands second in the hierarchy of attributes and was created in *Ahura Mazda*'s good mind.

(3) *Khshatra* is the third cardinal quality of God. No English word can explain it precisely and fully. *Khshatra* is a combination of holy, good, and constructive potentiality, power, influence, and hegemony. It should not be confused with physical strength. It represents true strength, sway, and authority. It denotes the divine kingdom. Divine power is the realization of *Ahura Mazda*'s will; it signifies the spiritual, mental, and moral strength that engenders love and not hatred, humility and not pride. *Khshatra* fosters in individuals a desire to serve others and not to oppress them.

(4) Universal Love and Tranquility, *Spenta Armaity*, indicates an inherent attitude of benevolence, vouchsafement, and love. It connotes loftiest dedication and selfless service. It implies love without expectation of reciprocity and dutifulness without contemplation of reward. It denotes the universal brotherhood of man.

(5) Perfection, *Haurvatat*, purports self-realization and wholeness. Sublime benevolence, creativity, and intelligence are features of *Ahura Mazda's* Perfection. *Haurvatat* is the highest state of goodness and excellence in this and the other world. It is often mentioned together with the sixth characteristic, *Ameretat* or immortality, in order to show the proximity and association of the two. Perfection also implies the absence of desire, expectation, or wish.

(6) Immortality, *Ameretat*, is the quality of eternity and of immutability. Life in its widest connotation is in God, with him and for him. He is not begotten, nor perishable and has no beginning and no end. Through him the universe exists and life is sustained. *Ameretat* is free from time and space.

With these attributes, the total goodness of *Ahura Mazda* is reaffirmed. As he does good exclusively, no evil can originate in him. Goodness being central to God, he cannot do evil. All that is complete and ideal is in him, with him, and emanates from him.

Ahura Mazda is the creator. It is the Source and has no origin. The words conveying that idea, used in the *Gathas*, are *Datar* and *Tashea*. The first word, *Datar*, derives from the root *Da*, meaning to give, bestow, and vouchsafe; and *Datar* means the giver. In this sense, all blessings are given by God and all that is good emanates from him. The second word, *Tashea*, stems from *Tash*, meaning to cut, shape, and design; and *Tashea* means shaper, designer, artisan, and maker. In this sense all creations are designed and made by God. Hence, in Zoroastrianism, creation implies a combination of giving and shaping, emanating and augmenting, designing and making. In Mazdaism, creation approximates emanation and all rays of light, beams of goodness, and radiant energies come from the Source-the Light of Lights.

Spenta Mainyu

Though not included in the six, *Spenta Mainyu* is another cardinal attribute of God. *Spenta Mainyu* is the Sublime Constructive power, the universal force of creativity and the essence of constructiveness and positivity. *Spenta* means growth and progress; *Mainyu* denotes mentality or spirit; the two words together mean "the augmenting spirit." Augmentation exists in both a quantitative and a qualitative sense. *Spenta Mainyu* is conceived in *Ahura Mazda's* mind and is sometimes called *Ahura Mazda's* son, symbolizing God's productivity. It is the self-realizing quality or activity of *Ahura Mazda*;[11] it is the self-generating energy that leads to the creation and evolution of the universe. *Spenta Mainyu* is dynamic and creation is an ongoing process. For Zoroaster, holiness meant also abundance, growth, and health.[12] *Spenta Mainyu* represents the principle of augmentation and development in the universe.

Creation is a component in the definition of *Ahura Mazda*; it is an aspect of *Ahura Mazda's* benevolence and vouchsafement. As such, creativity and creation are inherent and unintentional in *Ahura Mazda*. Creation, as an act of *Ahura Mazda, has an intrinsic* objective; and man's actions because of freedom of choice, are motivated. The consequences of man's free activities are governed by the law of *Asha. Ahura Mazda* has bestowed intelligence upon man and has given him freedom of choice to put *Ahura Mazda's* bounties to any use he chooses. Man reaps what he sows. Everything in its initial form is conducive to the good of mankind and the progress of the world. Man, however, may employ them for good or evil purposes. *Ahura Mazda* is the most beneficent spirit.[13]

The dignity, spirituality, and privity of *Ahura Mazda*, presented by Zoroaster, was an innovation in the ancient world. It was a new concept introduced in a new faith. Thenceforth for the

---

[11] Dhalla, 36. "*Spenta Mainyu* brings the transcendence and immanence of *Ahura Mazda* into synthesis; *Spenta Mainyu* is (God's) active working principle."

[12] Zaehner, *The Dawn*, 45.

[13] This is one of the distinctive features of Zoroaster's God. Unlike the Abrahimic religions, in which God can become angry or revengeful, Zoroaster's God is exclusively goodness. He cannot become angry and does not revenge.

Iranians, God became the Being of infinite morality, light, truth, and purity. God was to be served not by ceremonies but by virtuous acts, not by sacrifices but by selfless love, not by rituals but by good mind. Zoroaster presented God as moral perfection. He told people that *Ahura Mazda* is not revengeful but just and, therefore, should not be feared but loved, should not be abhorred but adored. *Ahura Mazda* does not need propitiation by rituals and sacrifices.[14]

Zoroaster proclaimed that *Ahura Mazda* is the author of everything good and all good things. *Ahura Mazda* is of infinite constructivity and power. Destruction does not emanate from him.

Ahura Mazda 's Existence

The Gathic approach to the issue of the existence of one God, *Ahura Mazda*, is intuitive, rational, and moral.

The little that is known about the beliefs of Indo-Iranians before the advent of Zoroaster indicates a primitive animism associated with the personification of natural phenomena, constituting a polytheistic creed. Zoroaster revolutionized existing beliefs, banned the multitude of deities, and preached monotheism-the existence of one invisible God who is the Spirit of Spirits, the Sublime Spirit, the Universal Spirit, the Universal Intelligence, the Universal Being and the Light of Lights. Zoroaster proclaimed that *Ahura Mazda*, known through his attributes, is worthy of worship to the exclusion of all imaginary gods. This was more than a mere reformation. How did Zoroaster arrive at that conclusion?

---

[14] In two passages in the *Gathas*, the use of the intoxicating drink (the cult *of Haoma*) is deplored: *Yasnas* 32-14, 48-10. Animal sacrifice was banned by Zoroaster. In Iranian mythology Yima fell from grace because of allowing the killing of ox. In *The Younger Avesta, mayazda* and *draonah* are used as ceremonial offerings. Because of the continuation of the cult of *Haoma*, Zaehner suggests that the filth of drink, which is condemned in *Yasna* 48-10, refers to its association with the sacrifice of animals. Zaehner, *The Teachings*, 127.

Through reason, Zoroaster doubted the truth and validity of the prevailing deities worshipped by the Indo-Iranian peoples; through intuitive cognition, good mind, and holy *Asha* he perceived *Ahura Mazda*. That was the beginning of his quest for truth. Such perception is accessible to those who verily seek the truth.[15]

Through a rational approach and practical reasoning, Zoroaster realized the logical necessity of the existence of an intelligent and hegemonic God. The graceful, uninterrupted round of day and night, the orderly course of the planets, the ceaseless seasonal succession, and the unfailing regularity of natural cycles point to the existence of a designer and sustainer–a creator. Reason indicates that such a creation with its regularity cannot be accidental, nor can it be the result of the concerted efforts of many deities.[16]

By employing the moral approach-practicing the qualities of truth, courage, and love-Zoroaster attained the divine power of self-realization and perfection; he was enabled to commune with God and see with his inner eye the reality of one God. He also realized that in their sublimity, those moral qualities were *Ahura Mazda*'s attributes that man must emulate.[17]

Thus Zoroaster, through the combined effort of mind, heart, and conscience; through mediation (*Tushna Maitih*), consultation with his good mind, practice of righteousness, and invocation of the Good Spirit (*Spenta Mainyu*) concluded that there must be a Sublime Reality, an Omniscient and Omnipresent God whom he called *Ahura Mazda*, the Lord of Wisdom and Being.[18]

---

[15] The *Gathas*: *Yasnas* 28-1, 2, 3, 4, 5, 6; 44-1.

[16] The *Gathas*: *Yasna* 44-3, 4, 5. Zoroaster is guided by *Vohu Mana* (Good Mind), who enlightens him that creation and sustenance of the world, earth, water, planets, seasonal order, etc., are the work of a sublime intelligence; creation and sustenance of the universe cannot be done by a group of deities. Also 32-2; 51-7.

[17] The *Gathas: Yasnas* 43-1, 2, 3, 5, 7; 44-7, 11, 15, 17; 28-5.

[18] The *Gathas*: *Yasna* 31-21,22 "May we through *Asha* be at one with Thee; May *mind and heart one pointed turn to Thee;* Whenever doubts our reason overwhelm." Also *Yasna* 43-4, 12.

Amesha Spenta

Amesha Spenta is the collective name used for the six cardinal attributes of *Ahura Mazda*. Only in two places in the *Gathas* are the six attributes of *Ahura Mazda* mentioned together and then without any collective name being ascribed to them.[19] The term *Amesha Spenta*, meaning Bounteous Immortals, first appeared in the *Haptan Ghaity*. While this assignation emphasized the great moral character of the faith, it also paved the way for the per- sonification of such attributes as archangels (administering agents of *Ahura Mazda*) in *The Younger Avesta*. *Amesha Spenta* shows the divine and absolute nature of morality in Zoroastrian religious philosophy. The six attributes are the creation and chil- dren of *Ahura Mazda*, a designation they retain throughout *The Younger Avesta*.[20] They are graceful, powerful, and wise. They assist *Ahura Mazda* in the sustenance of creation and the re- freshment of the universe.

In *The Younger Avesta*, each *Amesha Spenta* is identified with a physical element to which it gives protection. *Vohu Mana* watches over cattle, *Asha* over fire, *Khshatra* over metals, *Ar- maity* over earth, *Haurvatat* over water, and *Ameretat* over plants. Since God in the form of attributes appears in human be- ings, each of them is said to also perform a function in relation to the individual person and his body. Thus *Mana* guides the mind or mental riches, *Asha* health or bodily riches, *Khshatra* wealth or material riches, *Armaity* the heart or emotional riches, *Haur- vatat* conscience or self-fulfillment, and *Ameretat* eternal life; the best existence and communion is with *Ahura Mazda*.

Sometimes *Ahura Mazda* and his six attributes are called the seven *Amesha Spentas*, which merely indicates the oneness of the seven. The first seven days of the month in the Zoroastrian calendar are named after *Ahura Mazda* and his cardinal attrib- utes. (In the Zoroastrian calendar each month of thirty days is divided into four parts of eight and seven days alternately, corre- sponding to the four weeks in the present-day calendar. The first day in each week bears the name of God. The account of Genesis

---

[19] Dhalla, *History* 40, 162.
[20] In Pahlavi books, the Avestan *Ameshayaspenta* becomes *Amesha Spenta* and in Farsi becomes *Ameshaspand*, a term currently used by Zoroastrians in Iran.

that God created the world in six days does not appear in the *Gathas*. Hence the 'week' concept is not as relevant.)

"The development within the Jewish religion of such matters as angels, dualism, eschatology, and the resurrection of body is commonly attributed to the impact of Iranian religion," writes Professor James Barr. Professor Mary Boyce suggests that the idea of creation in the Old Testament arose through contact with Iran.[21] Although in the *Gathas* the attributes of *Ahura Mazda* are active and always in the scene, they do not play the role of separate entities as angels. As angels, one may say, they are on the margin and only to be assumed. It is in *The Yrounger Avesta* that as angels they become more pronounced and function as *Ahura Mazda*'s agents. Considering that man is also a coworker of God, the emergence of *Amesha Spentas and Yazatas* as angels–coworkers of God–in *The Younger Avesta* is not surprising. The difference between angels and man is seen in the fact that angels, as God's epithets, act always in accordance with *Ahura Mazda*'s will, whereas man, in the exercise of his freedom of choice, may deviate. The presumed role of the Magis, in the introduction of angels in *The Younger Avesta,* is described in the following.

Yazatas

Another group of personified virtues of *Ahura Mazda* are the *Yazatas*, which are, except for *Sraosha, Atar,* and *Ashi*, creations of *The Younger Avesta*. *Sraosha, Atar,* and *Ashi* are mentioned in the *Gathas*, but not as *Yazatas*. *Yazata* means adorable one. The adoration with which the *Yazatas* are invoked in the *Yashts* has become a matter of controversy. Some of the *Yazatas,* as helpers of *Ahura Mazda*, have acquired greater prominence than the *Amesha Spenta*, and their eulogization at times appears excessive. To illustrate this aberration, the case wherein *Ahura Mazda* himself presents an offering into the Y*azata Tishtrya* for more rain may be mentioned.[22] With the profundity behind the

---

[21] Quoted by Barr, 206.
[22] *Yasht*: 8. 20-29.

Y*azatas* and the historical background to it, such prodigality can be explained, if not excused.[23]

How did the concept of *Yazatas* enter *The Younger Avesta*? Let us recall that religion does not grow in a vacuum, and that its evolution is influenced by socio-political factors. The Achaemenians, whether dedicated Zoroastrians or not, proclaimed their devotion to *Ahura Mazda*. Parthians, though not Zoroastrians, displayed great inclination toward Zoroastrianism. Sassanians made tremendous use of their religion in their political enterprise. They made Zoroastrianism a legitimizing force for their rule and for demanding loyalty from their subjects.

A group that exerted great influence on the course and contents of the religious evolution during all this period seems to have been the Magis. Historical evidence indicates that before the Achaemenians, during the reign of the Medes, the priestly clan of Magis were politically and socially very powerful. In their religious practice, they were highly ritualistic, offering sacrifices to deities, interpreting dreams, reciting evil-dispelling spells, killing obnoxious creatures, and a host of other pursuits, all of which were reprobated by Zoroaster. For at least two reasons, Achaemenians could not have been favorable to the Magis: the Magis' religious practices and their close association with the Medes. Then came the advent of Guamata, who, through a well-organized plot, usurped the power and proclaimed himself King. He unsuccessfully tried to restore the position of the Magis. After Guamata's ouster by Darius, the Magis fell into complete disgrace. Realizing the firm establishment of the Achaemenian dynasty and the popular acceptance of Zoroastrianism, the Magis, who were reputed for their intellect and astuteness, chose to embrace Zoroastrianism and come to terms with the ruling class. The Magis were gradually rehabilitated. In the post-Darius era they managed to work their way up in the religious and political hierarchy and regain their lost social status. In the course of time the Magis succeeded in reintroducing some of the pre-Zoroastrian deities in the form of Y*azatas* into the new faith. The *Yazatas,* who were creations of God, acted as his administering officers. For socio-economic considerations, the Magis also re-

---

[23] Zaehner, 47. "Zarathushtra saw the spiritual and the material worlds as being the opposite poles of a unitary whole intimately linked together. The link is only weakened with the appearance of the Lie, and its representative *Angra Mainyu*, the destructive spirit."

introduced and linked some of the old rituals to the adorations of the *Yazatas*. Reidentification of *Yazatas* as attributes and creations of *Ahura Mazda*, in essence, was not incompatible with the Gathic principle that all good things emanated from, and were created by, *Ahura Mazda*. What constituted an aberration was the excessive glorification of *Yazatas*.

Some of the *Yazatas*, such as charity, piety, and peace, represent mental qualities; they are called *Mainyava*. Others, called *Gaethya*, represent material elements. *Gaethya* includes natural and atmospheric phenomena such as water, earth, fire, wind, sun, and moon. The ecological concern of the *Gathas* for the universe and its care for a healthy interrelationship between the human being and his environment explain the incentive for the inclusion of praise for, and glorification of, *Yazatas* in *The Younger Avesta*. It is not surprising that Mazdaism is called the first ecological religion. The reverence for *Yazatas* emphasizes the preservation of nature.[24] In that respect, the introduction of *Yazatas* into *The Younger Avesta* has served the purpose of bringing the importance of the protection of nature to the attention of all, particularly the populace, for whom religious commandments are more meaningful than scientific and governmental recommendations. Theologically too, the creation of *Yazatas* remains harmless inasmuch as *Ahura Mazda* continues to be the creator of all *Yazatas*, and thus his holiness remains unrivaled. The ethical and spiritual connotations of the *Yazatas* are immense; the Yazatas are perfect axiological vehicles. A brief description of the triad of *Sraosha*, *Rashnu*, and *Mitra*, as well as of *Yazatas Atar* and *Anahita* will demonstrate the point. The same cannot be said for the reintroduction of the rituals by the Magis.

The triad of *Sraosha*, *Rashnu*, and *Mitra*, the three-brother Yazatas, enjoy special prominence. They see to it that justice is done and that every individual receives the proper consequences of his or her actions. Sraosha represents God's all-hearing ears, Mitra represents God's all-seeing eyes, and Rashnu acts as the presiding judge, representing God's justice. With such a construction of court no fact can be hidden or undisclosed. Conse-

---

[24] *Yasnas* 1-19, 3-4, 7-4, 16-9; Yashts 6-3, 4, 10-13. *Mainyava* and *Gaethya*, matter and spirit, and all other things created by God are good.

quently, perfect justice is assured. Undoubtedly, the metaphor is beautiful and impressive.

In addition to their judicial function, Sraosha and Mitra perform other duties. Sraosha is the revelation channel, the religious teacher, and the watcher of man's body and soul. He is as much God's ear as he is the "universal ear" of the entire righteous people. Equating God's ear or eye to those of an entire righteous people points to the spiritual oneness of righteous people and God. Thus Sraosha serves as a two-way channel: conveying God's message to mankind and transmitting the message of the righteous to God. Mitra is the genius of the sanctity of the contract and the foe of falsehood. He conducts the divine struggle against evil and chastises those in breach of promise.

Three *Yazatas*, *Apam Napat*, *Anahita*, and *Ahurani* look after the water and the two *Yazatas Atar* and *Neryosang* after the fire; *Vayu* is the genius of wind and *Zam* of earth. Thus the four traditional elements of nature receive special attention, portraying the sanctity of nature. The care for nature is a religious duty, and destruction of the material world is a sin. The individuals who do not observe this duty will be watched and chastised by the respective *Yazatas*.

Of the three *Yazatas* for water, *Apam Napat* is male and the other two are female. *Apam Napat*, the chief genius of water, lives beneath the waters, and in cooperation with *Vayu*, the genius of wind, distributes water on earth.[25] In the course of time, *Apam Napat* lost his prominence to *Anahita*, believed to be a non-Indo-Iranian goddess. The word *Anahita* means undefiled and implies that the water should be kept clean. *Anahita* is also the bestower of fertility and the facilitator of childbirth. In order to make the genius of water happy, one must do one's utmost to keep the water clean. *Ahurani* looks after *Vourukasha* (the sea) and other waters. Besides, she brings health, wealth, and fame to those who keep the water clean.

Atar means fire, light, and the flame of fire. Symbolically it represents the eternal light of *Ahura Mazda*. The Indo-Iranian reverence for fire was retained by Zoroaster and stressed by the Magis. Fire is venerated in all religions. In Christianity, God is characterized as "the consuming fire;"[26] in Islam Allah is "the

---

[25] *Yasht* 8-34.
[26] The Epistle of Paul to the Hebrew, ch. 12-28.

light of sky and earth;"[27] and in Judaism Yahweh descended in fire upon Mount Sinai.[28] In Zoroastrianism, good mentality and truth are symbolized by light, and falsehood by darkness; God is described as the Sublime Light; and heaven interchangeably is referred to as the Abode of Light, the Abode of Good Mind, and the Abode of Best Existence. As the flame of fire travels upward, human beings should improve themselves in order to progress in life. The concept of God and goodness as light has a profound significance in Mazdaism as has the color white. In all religious ceremonies, be it initiations of youth into faith, marriages, or memorial (funeral) services, Zoroastrians wear white clothes. In their prayers they look to the light, be it sun, moon, or fire light. In *The Younger Avesta, Atar* is called the great *Yazata* who, in association with *Nairyosangha,* acts as guardian to fire.

The two other natural elements, earth and air, are represented by *Zam* and *Vayu*. The latter means the movement of air or wind. *Zam*, the guardian of earth, is also called *Zamyat*. *Vayu*, the genius of the wind, is divided into two parts, one of which is productive and the other destructive. In *Avesta*, only the good part, which is strong and firm, is adored as a good-doer, vanquisher, and smiter of the evil. Thus the three male *Yazatas* of *Atar, Anahita*, and *Vayu* are protectors of fire, water and air and the female *Yazata* of *Zam* is guardian of earth, all of whom are sanctified.

The names of several other *Yazatas* mentioned in the holy scriptures are: *Hvarekhshaeta*, Sun; *Maonghah*, moon; *Vanat*, star; *Asman*, sky; *Sirus Tishtra*, rain; *Ushta*, dawn; and *Anaghra Raosha*, light. *Haoma* is another important *Yazata*. It was the plant used in the pre-Zoroastrian era in the religious ceremonies; and having resumed its function in *Yasna* ritual in *The Younger Avesta,* it was elevated to the position of *Yazata* and still is symbolically used in the rites. In *The Younger Avesta,* certain other bounties of God such as *Airyaman*, health; *Daena*, conscience; *Chisti*, knowledge; *Rata*, charity; *Akhshti*, peace; *Ashi*, piety; and *Verethraghnam*, victory, are also *yazat*ized.

Personification of *Yazatas* in *The Younger Avesta* resulted in the emergence of the angels. This new development led some

---

[27] Koran: Light 35.
[28] Exodus: ch. 19-18, 19, 20; ch. 34-4, 5, 6.

writers erroneously to designate Ohrmozd a godhead, which is not justified.

Yazatas are not gods; they are coworkers of Ohrmozd inasmuch as human beings are, though without free choice and temptation to do evil acts!

Dualism

Some scholars have suggested that by admitting two primordial spirits – Good and Evil – Zoroastrianism is a dualist religion. Zoroastrians have reacted sharply to this contention. The discord is substantive, not merely semantic, contrary to the view of the Catholic Bishop, Dr. Casartelli, who states that "the question of dualism in Zoroastrianism is one of terms."[29]

The world religions are divided roughly into two groups: Abrahamic and Eastern. The Abrahamic religions are monotheistic. For all practical purposes, a religion is considered monotheistic if (i) it believes in, and worships, one God-Creator-Sustainer, who is transcendent and eternal; (ii) it believes in the prophethood, revelation, and holy scripture that contains God's message. and (iii) it believes in life after death, reward, and punishment.

In contrast, great Eastern religions such as Hinduism, Buddhism, and their sister religious traditions, are not, strictly speaking, monotheistic. In the Eastern religions, practiced by half of the world population, the demarcation line between divine and human, real and imaginary, history and mythology, is not clear-cut. Hinduism was not revealed to a particular prophet, and according to its followers, the religion is primordial and always was. Hindu's Brahman is the Ultimate Reality conceived of as one and undifferentiated, static, and dynamic, and beyond all definitions. It is not God. It is expressed as *neti neti*, meaning neither this nor that. It is neither good nor bad, neither constructive nor destructive, neither transcendent nor immanent. Its name and description is silence. Brahman is a mythical image. In Hinduism, gods have earthly incarnations, and Krishna, a warrior

---

[29] Duchesne-Guillemin, *"The Western Response,"* 7.

god, for instance, is the incarnation of the god Vishnu. He himself is a divine figure. A similar situation exists with Buddhism. Buddhism does not believe in God, in personal spirit, or in revelation. Nevertheless the Eastern religions in an ambiguous manner believe in some impersonal spirit as Godhead.

Within these two broad categories, differences exist regarding God's qualities, God's manifestation, God's relationship to man, and creation. The idea of the Trinity, for instance, is repulsive to Muslims; whereas the Muslim idea of the revengefulness of God is unacceptable to Christianity. Karma, in Hinduism, as the effect of any action upon the doer-whether in a past existence or in the present–represents a blind determinism; whereas in Buddhism every being, while inheriting the karmas of the past lives, can change its fate by free will. In Jainism, karma is something that binds the individual to the attractions of the material world. Thus, we see that concepts presented under the same label, by religions within the same division, differ in content.

Believing in the basic tenets of monotheistic religions-the transcendence and eternity of the creator, revelation, God's message, and life after death with reward and punishment–Zoroastrianism must be classified as a monotheistic religion. This, however, should not imply that the nature and attributes of Zoroaster's God or the process of revelation or prophethood in Zoroastrianism necessarily tally in details with those in any of the Abrahamic religions. This should not be surprising. Moses' Yahweh and Mohammed's Allah represent gods of two monotheistic religions; so does the Christian doctrine of the Trinity, which in form is different from that of Judaism and Islam. Yet Christianity is considered as monotheistic as the other two. So it is with Zoroaster's *Ahura Mazda* and with the eternal, omniscient, and omnipotent Ohrmozd, who finally triumphs over Ahriman.

To say that Zoroastrians are dualist is one thing; to say that they are dyrotheist is another. Zoroastrians do not believe in two Gods and thus are not dyotheists. Zoroastrianism may be considered dualist within the context of monotheism. *Ahura Mazda* created the earthly and the heavenly worlds (*astvant* and *manahya*) in his exclusive goodness; dualism is represented in creation through the manifestation of the opposites to the creation of God in the form of *tweens*. The tweens have a beginning an and end, Ahura Mazda has none. Monotheism is ingrained in the

Gathas in the most unambiguous terms and described throughout the holy scripture, as seen in the following two passages:

> *Verily, I believe Thee*, O Mazda Ahura, *to be* the Supreme Benevolent Providence,
> *For I beheld Thee as the* Primeval Cause *of all creation,*
> *For by Thy* Perfect Wisdom *Thou shall render just*
> *   recompense for all actions,*
> *good to good, evil to evil,*
> *till the last day of creation.*
>   (Gathas: Yasna 43–5)

> *Where is the faithful man who heeds me as the first*
> *   To teach*
> *That, verily, Thou art the Highest to invoke,*
> *In very deed, the Bountiful Providence,*
> *   The Holy Lord!*
> *Who will hear, through the Good Mind*
> *What Truth made known to me,*
> *The Truth revealed by the Creator Supreme!*
>   (Gathas: Yasna 46-9)

Nothing can detract from the monotheistic character of Zoroastrianism; nothing can disparage the profundity of dualism in that faith. If in theology monotheism is the evolution of polytheism; in philosophy dualism seems to be the evolution of monoism. However in this book we are concerned primarily with the doctrinal beliefs of a faith and not with value judgment–the merit of one concept over another. Some argue that Zoroastrianism believes in cosmic dualism; others maintain that Zoroastrianism believes in theological monotheism and ethical dualism; but all concede that Zoroastrianism is primarily an "ethical religion". The ethical and creative manifestation of God in *Spenta Mainyu* has given rise to the controversy.

To conclude, Zoroastrianism believes in one creator-sustainer of the universe; he is the source of being, he is omniscient, omnipresent, and omnipotent; he is the only one worthy of worship; he is without beginning and end, unchanging and eternal, who appears only in his attributes; he created the universe in his good mind (*Vahishta Mana*), shaped it in his conscience (*Daena*), manifested it through his benevolent spirit (*Spenta Mainyu*), and set it into motion by his will (*Asha Vahishta*)-the eternal law of justice and righteousness; he created man as his coworker and friend with faculties to discern between right and wrong and to work for the advancement of the universe; he revealed his eternal law to the prophet Zoroaster in the *Gathas*; he proclaimed the law of consequences and the reality of the life hereafter; and he prescribed true happiness (*Ushta*) for the righteous. In our time, the practicing men and women, wherever they are, continue to invoke *Ahura Mazda* as the only God in the Gathic tradition, with a humble, grateful heart and uplifted hands. They continue to pray through the righteous acts of *Asha*, the good wisdom of *Vohu Mana*, and the love and dedication of *Armaity*, that the benevolent spirit of *Ahura Mazda* may grant them the perfect bliss of *Haurvatat* and the divine power of *Khshatra* to bring solace to the soul of the universe and to immortalize themselves.

II

THE PROPHETHOOD OF ZOROASTER

The Principle of Revelation

Thus spake Ahura Mazda:-
"The one, who alone has hearkened to my precepts
   is known as Zarathushtra Spitama,
For his Creator and for Truth, he wishes to announce
   the Holy Message,
Wherefore shall I bestow upon him the gift of eloquent speech."
(Gathas: Yasna 29-8)

Revelation

Mazdaism is a revealed religion. It is God's message and Zoroaster is God's prophet. Yet in Mazdaism the role of the prophet was not only the communication of a message. The prophet was also a forerunner and a herald who went through a tirelessly laborious trial then reached the state of perfection. Zoroaster's prophetic mission was a two-way process. It consisted of a period of theosophic contemplation by Zoroaster followed by God's revelation. It was Zoroaster who initiated the process and proved himself worthy of the mission. His holiness, righteousness, and positivity had earned him *Ahura Mazda's* trust, and in his omniscience, *Ahura Mazda* knew of Zoroaster's willingness to announce and spread his holy message.

    The process of appointment to prophethood is the only part of Zoroaster's life story that is documented in the *Gathas*, the holy scriptures. This is not surprising. Gathic Mazdaism is against all cults, including the cult of personality. No information about Zoroaster's genealogy or immediate family are incorporated in the *Gathas,* except that he belonged to the *Spitama* clan or household. In the holy scripture the name of one of his daughters is also mentioned, not for the reason of consanguinity, but because she was one of the first active disciples of the prophet. However, an account of the prophet's family tree is given in *The Younger Avesta.*

In the Gathic account of the prophet's ministry three distinct stages are discernable. First is the milieu of the young Zoroaster's doubt and dismay. Zoroaster discredits the generally believed views on the deities and their assumed jurisdictions. He negates the teachings of the *Athravans* and *Magis* on the reality and purpose of life.

Zoroaster was born of virtuous parents and had been brought up in the Indo-Iranian religious environment of a pantheon of deities. Early in life he questioned the truth of gods and goddesses. He was appalled at the practice of animal sacrifice and the use of intoxicating drinks in religious rites.[1] He disapproved of self-centered clergies and their practice of exorcism. He abhorred the clergy's greed and their capitalization on people's superstitious convictions. Early in life, Zoroaster sensed a fundamental inadequacy in the socio-religious structure of the community. He perceived human misery to be the natural consequence of errancy in human deeds. He then set out to discover the rightness, the truth, and the mystery of happiness, through observation, the application of a holy intellect, the practice of meditation, and intuitive cognition.[2]

The second step consisted of Zoroaster's inquiry into Ultimate Truth. His approach was intuitive, rational, and moral; in the process both his mind and conscience were activated. At the rational level, by observing the rounds of day and night, the course of the planets, the seasonal succession, and the complex structure in nature and human, Zoroaster concluded that there must be a

---

[1] The *Gathas: Yasnas* 32-14; 46-11; 48-10 In these passages the prophet reproaches Karapans (the priests) and Kavis (the princes) who wilfully mislead people.

[2] The *Gathas: Yasnas* 43-15 (observation and reasoning), 44-3, 4, 5, 7; 28-2, 5, 6, (reasoning and intuition). Silent meditation, *Tushma Maitih* is recommended.

supporting intelligent force which designs and regulates such a scheme. He pondered that such an intricate and orderly set-up can happen neither by accident nor by creation on the part of a group of independent and equally ranked deities. He reasoned in his holy mind, *Mana*, that the unfailing order of creation must be the work of one great and powerful Monad which is infinite and indefinable by finite man. He further considered creation in its universality as a manifestation of Ultimate Reality. He called that Universal Intelligence, *Vahishta Mana* (the Sublime Wisdom), and postulated that the Sublime Wisdom was the author of creation and that creation proceeds according to the law of *Asha*. He visualized the Creator as possessor of the holy divine power that he called *Khshatra*. Having formulated a prima facie concept of God through God's attributes, Zoroaster was eager to perceive him through the eyes of his mind and conscience. He longed to see the author of the eternal law, the designer of the universe, and the cause of creation. He had pondered that except through attributes, a finite man cannot see and comprehend the Infinite; he discerned that Sublime Wisdom must be the first attribute of the True God. He was determined to have communion with God. Listening to the call of his conscience, *Daena*, he realized that such a communion is possible only at a moral level, the level of *Asha* or righteousness. This realization is recorded in the *Gathas*:

> O Asha, *equipped with the knowledge of Truth and*
>   Righteousness
> *When shall I see Thee, and* Vohu-Mana *too!*
> *And through that Inspiration* (Sraosha), *when shall I*
>   *Be in the presence of the Most*
>   *Beneficent* Mazda!
> *With the proclamation of these sacred words shall*
> *We make the evil ones turn towards*
> *Thee* O Holy Mazda!
>
> (Gathas: Yasna 28–5)

Operating at the level of *Asha* with all its moral and ethical implications, was the third stage. Zoroaster trod the path of righteousness with precision, practicing selfless love, moral courage, and truth in all of its facets, in pursuit of the good mind and invoking the Holy Spirit.

Zoroaster emulated God's attributes. He dedicated all of his life to the preaching of truth, the guidance of his fellow human beings, and the preservation of nature. Zoroaster, apostrophizing the Holy Spirit, communed with the Good Mind, ascended the Path of Truth, consummated Universal Love, acquired Divine Courage, attained Self-Realization, and thus became Perfect and Immortal.[3] With his mind's eye he saw God, in his conscience he felt God and from being with him, Zoroaster derived the greatest of joy. Every day he gained a deeper insight into the nature of Ultimate Reality.

Concurrent with the process of Zoroaster's inquiry into the Truth, but quite at a different plateau, the Soul of Creation, *Geush Urvan,* complained to God about the spread of injustice, violence, hatred, hostility and revenge on earth. She indicted the ravaging disharmony in society. She entreated God for help. She craved to cleanse the earth of destructive elements. Conscious of the destination of the creation, she implored the Creator to send a strong and righteous individual to rectify the situation and to re-store peace, accord, and progress to the world.[4] Her request was vouchsafed by Righteousness and thus was considered by God.

> *Unto Thee, O Lord, the Soul of Creation cried*
> *For whom didst Thou create me and who*
>   *so fashioned me?*
> *Feuds and fury, violence and the insolence*
>   *of might, have oppressed me.*
> *None have I to protect me save Thee,*
> *Command for me, then, the blessings of a settled,*
>   *peaceful life.*
>
>   (Gathas: Yasna 29–1)

Having counseled with his Sublime Mind and his Righteousness on the complaint of the Soul of Creation, *Ahura Mazda* declared his will. This account confirms the indispensability of the counsel of Holy Mind and Conscience for man before embarking on any course of action.

---

[3] The *Gathas: Yasna* 28-1, 2, 3, 4, 5, 6; Zoroaster sees God with the eyes of his soul, *Yasna* 45-8.
[4] The *Gathas: Yasna* 29-1 to 8.

The *Gathas* inform us that *Ahura Mazda*, in response to the request by the Soul of Creation (or Mother Earth), appointed Zoroaster as his prophet.

> *Then, thus spake Ahura Mazda, the Lord of*
> *understanding and wisdom:*
> *"As there is no righteous spiritual lord or secular*
> *chief,*
> *So have I, as Creator, made thee (Zarathushtra) the*
> *protector and guide,*
> *For the welfare of the world and its diligent people."*
> (Gathas: Yasna 29–6)

Taken aback by Ahura Mazda's announcement, the Soul of Creation pleaded:

> *Thereupon the Soul of Creation cried:*
> *"In my woes I have obtained for help the feeble*
> *voice of an humble man,*
> *When I wished for a mighty over-lord!*
> *Whenever shall I get one to give me help with power*
> *And with force?"*
> (Gathas: Yasna 29–9)

Thereupon Ahura Mazda decleared: "one such person is well-known to me and he is Zarathushtra Spenta. He is the one who has listened to our Commands and put them into practice. He is also eager to proclaim through songs and hymms, the Holy Message and Eternal Low of Asha. Hence I shall grant him the sweetness of speech to carry out his mission."

Then Ahura Mazda revealed his message (*Manthra*) to Zoroaster. The voice of God was transmitted through Sraosha, personified as the teacher of religion. God's voice was heard by Zoroaster through his mind's ears.[5] The metaphors used are beautiful and revealing. This all happened in an abstract and spiritual ambiance where no physical movement was involved.

---

[5] The *Gathas: Yasnas* 29-8, 44-1, 43-7, 8, 11, 12. The communication with God is through good mind, and Zoroaster finds goodness through love.

Once Zoroaster received the message, he pledged "to teach that which was revealed to him in the very words of the Most Holy,[6] the Hymns contained in the *Gathas*."[7]

The account of the prophetic mission recorded in the *Gathas is* rational and at the same time occult. It embodies the fundamentals of good religion. In the process, reason and intuition are interwoven, mind and conscience are united, and all moral forces are at work to have the Words of Truth revealed to the prophet.[8]

Gathas

The *Gathas* are God's teachings in sweet hymns, *Manthras. Gathas* means Holy hymns and *Manthras* means thought-provoking. They constitute the rules of the best life and are God's eternal law. Their goal is the removal of inequity and injustice. They are conducive to the development and progress of the world. The *Gathas* exemplifies the fullness of perfection, the luminousness of divine Wisdom, the felicitousness of the faith of Truth, and the consequential blessings of Goodness. It displays the process of Refreshment, Frash–Kreti, the establishment of divine Sovereignty, *Khshatra,* on earth.

The *Gathas* are rational, practical, and universal

Firstly, the *Gathas* are rational.[9] Holy reason is a constant thread running throughout the *Gathas*. Sublime Mind (or Wis-

---

[6] The *Gathas*: *Yasnas* 34-6, 15; 43-8; 45-3; 54-2.

[7] The *Gathas*: *Yasna* 51-2 to 8. Zoroaster pays homage to the Holy Words. The *Gathas*. which is fulness of perfection. The *Daeva* worshippers try to corrupt it, *Yasna* 51-10. The Righteousness, including *Maidyo imangha*, propagate God's laws as they are revealed in the *Gathas*; the effective mode of the propagation of the faith is the emulation of God's attributes and selfless service to others, *Yasna* 51-19, 22.

[8] The *Gathas*: *Yasna* 30-7 to 9. In Zoroastrianism, the triad of mind, heart, and conscience must work in unison in order to produce wisdom, love, and justice-the requirement of the law of *Asha, Yasna* 43-12.

[9] The *Gathas*: *Yasna* 30-1, 2. Holy Wisdom (Mind or Reason) is a constant thread running through the *Gathas*. The Lord of Wisdom is God's name; God conceived the universe in his Wisdom; Wisdom is the first quality and creation of (or emanation from) God; the second attribute of God, *Asha,* was created in God's Wisdom and so were the other attrib-

dom) is the first mentioned quality of God. *Ahura Mazda* conceived the universe in his Sublime Mind. He consulted his mind and righteousness before choosing Zoroaster as a prophet. Zoroaster perceived God in his good mind. Man's personality is made substantially by the divine might of his or her mind. The prophet invites his audience to listen to his sermons and weigh them with their good minds and reasoning. He insists upon their making their choice rationally. Also the *Gathas* speak of *Khratu*, inherent intelligence, and *Chisti*, acquired knowledge, thus emphasizing the importance of learning.

Secondly, the *Gathas* are practical.[10] They teach mankind to lead an active life based on good thoughts, good words, and good deeds for the happiness of all and for the progress and renovation of the world. The rules of morality make up the main body of the *Gathas*. They direct man's way of life in a most simple and practical manner. Rather than being concerned with theological intricacies, the *Gathas* are concerned with the meaning of right and wrong and with the formation of a moral judgment. The *Gathas* were revealed to guide man through divine Wisdom, to advance the world through unity and humane deeds, and to obliterate misery and degradation in man. The *Gathas* are the first ecological law. Man as a coworker of God must respect the sanctity of nature and work for its preservation and sustenance. The maxims of good thoughts, *Humata;* good words, *Hukhta;* and good deeds, *Huvarshta;* are the most comprehensively practical rules of behavior ever stated.

The *Gathas* are universal.[11] According to the *Gathas*, their message contains the highest truths for all mankind. Zoroaster

---

utes; For Zoroaster, Good Mind was the first means of communication with God; Man makes his choice between good and bad through mind; heaven is the eternal abode of good mind.

[10] The *Gathas* are a code of life; the greater portion of them are concerned with ethics. Theology forms the smaller part of the *Gathas,* and the rituals too. The three maxims of Good Thought, Good Word, and Good Deed are the most practically comprehensive code of moral life ever formulated.

[11] The *Gathas*: *Yasna* 45-5. Zoroaster says, "I will teach that which was revealed to me and is best for *mortals* (all human beings)"; *Yasna* 43-1. "I will explain the (religion) to *all of you* who come *from near and far to listen.*" *Yasna* 49-3. "It is laid down by *Ahura Mazda* that *everybody* must have the choice *to choose these teachings.*" The Gathic

preaches for everybody without distinction of race, color, or sex. His aim is the universal uplift of truth, the promotion of love, harmonization of mind and heart, the self-realization of man, and the attainment of happiness, *Ushta.*[12] The universality of religion is evident in that Zoroaster addresses all mankind without any ethnic, racial, or other distinctions. He speaks for all who have come from near and far to listen to him preach. He declares that he has come to convert all into the new faith; yet he promises to all mankind the bliss of good deeds.[13] Righteousness to Zoroaster was synonymous with Mazdaism. The imperative was righteousness and virtue, and whoever was virtuous, *Ashu,* would enjoy the euphoria promised in the *Gathas.*[14] Social, rather than theological considerations explain the current reluctance of the practicing Zoroastrian to accept non-born-Zoroastrians into their fold. In Iran, Muslims could not embrace Zoroastrianism or else they would be exposed to the death penalty. Islamic society is a closed society; everybody can join in, but nobody can leave. In India, the Parsees who immigrated to India in the ninth century promised the ruler of Gujurat that they would not interfere with Hindu beliefs. They have honored their promise. In modern times, socio-economic considerations and the survival issue are cited as additional reasons for non-conversion. The whole question of acceptance of non-born-Zoroastrians into the faith has turned into a hot and damaging controversy which will finally resolve itself by the exigencies of modernity and mobility.

In Zoroastrianism virtue means justice. Virtue does not denote the blind performance of what is ordered and refrainment from what is forbidden; it connotes that man's acts of commission and omission must result in justice. In this context one's

---

word *Ahmai,* used in these passages, is a demonstrative pronoun, meaning each one, everybody and all. This points to the universality of religion. Furthermore, the prophet addresses his disciples to preach the religion of Truth to all mankind. *Yasna* 51-17, 19, 20.

[12] The *Gathas: Yasna* 43-1, 3. Whoever works for the happiness of others receives happiness (*Ushta*). *Yasnas* 30-2; 45-1.

[13] The *Gathas: Yasna* 43-1, 2, 3, 7, 14. God promised the bliss of good deeds to all Ashvans (righteous and just persons).

[14] The *Gathas: Yasna* 50-2, 3, 4. Those who work for the development and advancement of the world will receive God's bliss.

intentions and the results of one's action assume relevance.[15] The prophet proclaims that he is teaching what he has learned from *Ahura Mazda* and he is teaching to all who wish to listen to the words of Truth and enjoy a happy life.

> *Tell me*, O Mazdz –
> *That which Thou shalt bestow by Thy Spirit and*
>   *Inner Fire*
> *The blessing Thou shalt assign through Truth for*
>   *those acting with discernment,*
> *The Holy Law for their enlightenment*
> *All that to us, O Mazda, clear explain,*
> *Give it in Thy own inspired word*
> *That I may thereby bring its realization to all.*
>   (Gathas:Yasna 31–3)

In proselytization, no compulsion, no threat, and no force should be used. No material motive-wealth, marriage, or other worldly, mundane things-should influence one's decision to accept a faith. In the light of the requirements of faith as explained in the *Gathas*, it would be correct to say that Mazdaism is a matter of acceptance and not conversion.

Zoroaster was an exceptionally wise and holy person. God had given him, according to the *Gathas*, the charm of speech so that he would convert people by tongue and not by sword.

The *Gathas*'s concern for the dignity of man, both as an individual and a member of society; for the equality of male and female, and, indeed, of all human beings, is striking. The superiority of one individual over another depends solely on the degree of one's righteousness. The *Gathas* divide people into two groups, *Ashvan*, the righteous; and *Dregvant*, the wicked. Being a Zoroastrian only in name-by a mere declaration of faith-is not sufficient. Deed, not word, is the test.

Zoroaster yearns for the brotherhood of Ashvan, *Magha*, that would gladden the conscience of men and women of Zoroastrian

---

[15] Cf. those religions in which an oral admission of the faith is sufficient. In Zoroastrianism the intent and the state of mind is important. *Yasna* 30-5. Zoroastrians in their daily prayers recite: "I profess myself to be a *Mazda* worshipper, a follower of Zoroaster, acting in accord with the law of *Asha* and turning away from evil," *Khordeh Avesta*, *Sraosha Baj*; the Gathas state that the act of worship is by deed, not by words. *Yasna* 51-19.

faith. He emphasizes that *Ahura Mazda* gives his blessings to all righteous souls who cooperate with, *Ahura Mazda* in the establishment of the *Khshatra* on earth.[16] The Gathic concept of the brotherhood of man provides an additional testimony to the universality of the faith.

The *Gathas* are not a book of expediency, and the instructions therein are not for particular circumstances at particular points in time.[17] The principles contained in the *Gathas* are of a general nature. They are applicable to all individuals at all times and places, irrespective of peripherally extraneous differences. Even the prophet is subject to the same rules. God's act of creation takes place according to the same law, which is God's will. Emphasizing the point, we may assert that there is one law –God's law– to which God and human beings alike are subject. The predominance of the law of *Asha* in the *Gathas* is unmistakable. According to this law, righteousness and wickedness, truth and falsehood can never be reconciled, and no compromise between the two is permissible. Accordingly, the concept of a "white lie" or "lie of expediency" is false. (The concept of ideal truth or Asha will be discussed in the next chapter on Asha.) Goodness and evil are estranged and as such "peaceful coexistence" between the two is not feasible. There is also a distinction between "apparent" and "real or ideal" truth. *Asha* denotes ideal truth that is real and absolutely etichal. This clear and unequivocal approach manifests itself in a unique consistency throughout the *Gathas*. Because of the preponderance of the law of *Asha,* connoting progress, on the one hand; and the instrumentality of *Spenta Mainyu*, denoting augmentation and development, on the other hand, no theological clash between the Gathic principles and modernity occurs, so long as modernity does not transgress the principles of Zoroastrian morality. The dynamism of the Gathic rules answers the issues posed by the changing times. The two laws of development and progress, as corollaries of the law of oneness and creation, guarantee the desired harmony.

---

[16]The *Gathas*: *Yasna* 51-22. All Ashavan are worthy of reverance. The best act of worship is performed by he who acts righteously.

[17] Cf. with Koran in which contradiction is explained by reference to the occasion on which each passage (*Ayeh*) is revealed. The *Gathas* are a coherent body of rules.   Divergences between the *Gathas* and *TheYounger Avesta* should be resolved in favor of the *Gathas*.

Zoroaster

In addition to the account of Zoroaster's appointment to prophethood, the *Gathas* give the names of seven of the prophet's early disciples. Two of them happen to be related to the prophet by consanguinity. *Maidyoimaongha*, the first disciple, was the prophet's cousin and *Pouruchista* was his daughter. *Frashaoshtra* and *Jamaspa*, two brothers of the Hvoga clan, *Fryana*, of the Turanian ethnic group, Kay *Vishtaspa*, and his royal consort, *Hutaosa*, are other early disciples named in the *Gathas*.[18] The *Gathas* contain certain instructions by the prophet to his disciples concerning the manner in which they should live, preach, and be exemplary to others. The sermon of Zoroaster on the occasion of his daughter's marriage to Frashaoshtra is an important document on the equality of sexes. It emphasizes a woman's freedom in choosing her consort. In the *Gathas* women are treated always on an equal footing with men.[19]

In the introduction to this book, we offered an explanation for the omission in the *Gathas* of the prophet's genealogy. *The Younger Avesta*, however, gives the names of his parents as *Pourushaspa* (his father) and *Dughdhova* (his mother).[20] It is mentioned that both of them belonged to highly respected families prominent for their piety.

The Younger Avesta also informs us that by the time the young Zoroaster reached fifteen, he had learned all that he could about the mysteries of creation and the realities of life from the sages of his time. His inquisitive mind, however, had not been satisfied and his divine intelligence knew no boundaries. So he turned to meditation and self-investigation. He aimed at self-realization and understanding of the role of man in creation. For

---

[18] The *Gathas*: *Yasnas* 28-8, 4616, 49-8, 51-17, 53-2 (*Frashaoshtra*); *Yasnas* 28-7, 46-f14, 51-16, 53-2 (*Vishtasp*); *Yasnas* 46-17,49-f19, 51-18 (*Jamaspa*), *Yasnas* 51-19, 53-2 *Maidyo Mah* = *Maidyo imangha*; *Yasna* 53-3 (*Pouru Chista*); *Yasna* 46-12 (*Fryana*).

[19] The *Gathas*: *Yasnas* 30-2, 46-10, 53-5 to 9. The *Gathas* treat man and woman alike; everywhere man and woman are addressed on the same footing.

[20] *Vendidad* 19-4; Dinkard, in *Sacred Books of the East*. vol.37, book 8.14.1, 31; vol. 47, book 7.2.2-10, 17-19.

fifteen years the virtuous Zoroaster trod the path of truth and continued his meditation, counseling with the Good Mind, Conscience, and the Holy Love. At the age of thirty, he received his mission. During the first twelve years of his ministry, the prophet was constantly rebuked in his hometown of Chaychast. He was vexed with the insolent defiance of the ruling princes and priests but he did not default. He was resolute in his mission, firm in his stand, and confident in the ultimate triumph of Truth. An account of this episode of the prophet's life is given in the *Gathas*. At one point the prophet complained that the rulers held to falsehood, threatened him, and separated his followers from him. Then he asked Ahura to what land he should migrate.

> *To what land shall I turn, and whither turning shall I go?*
> *For my kinsmen and my peers have deserted me.*
> *Not the people, nor their wicked rulers, favor me.*
> *How shall I satisfy Thee, O Ahura Mazda?*
>
> (Gathas: Yasna 46–1)

> *I know, Mazda, why I am a man foiled in his wish.*
> *I have but only a few with me, and scantier still are*
>   *My means for their support.*
> *Behold, my Lord, I address my appeal to Thee,*
> *Grant me Thy gracious help, as a friend might give*
>   *To a friend.*
> *Grant me, through Truth, the acquisition of the*
>   *riches of the Good Mind.*
>
> (Gathas: Yasna 46–2)

At the age of forty-two, Zoroaster, along with several of his disciples, left his hometown and migrated to Bactria in eastern Iran. Continuing with his proselytization, the prophet again was confronted by the self-interested social parasites who jealously and provocatively tried to retain their privileged positions in that society. The news of the new prophet reached Kavi Vishtasp, the local king in Balkh, who invited Zoroaster to his palace to explain his beliefs. He also invited his high priests to be present and to argue their viewpoints based on their traditional faith. Witnessing the force of Zoroaster's presentations and the soundness of his doctrines, Vishtasp reproached the traditional priests for their animosity toward the prophet, and himself embraced the new religion, despite contrary advice by his courtiers. This event was a turning point in the history of the new religion. At the same time it set into motion a new wave of opposition by the traditional priests and ruling princes against the prophet. In the *Gathas* the prophet reproaches the princes and priests who with their evil deeds try to keep mankind in yoke.[21]

> *The Karpans and the Kavis have tyrannized over*
>   *Humanity,*
> *Their evil actions are destructive of Life.*
> *Verily, the conscience of such a one shall torment*
>   *His soul.*
> *And thus, when they shall come to the Bridge of*
>   *Judgment,*
> *Their abode, for endless ages, shall be in the House*
>   *Of the Lie.*
> (Gathas: Yasna 46–11)

> *The teacher of evil destroys the Understanding,*
> *He destroys the design of life,*
> *Snatches away the blessed realization of the Good*
>   *Mind.*
> *With these deeply felt words proceeding from my*
>   *Spirit,*
> *I cry to Thee, O Mazdz, and the Spirit of Truth!*
> (Gathas: Yasna 32–9)

Notwithstanding tremendous difficulties, Zoroaster pledges his dedication to continue preaching the truth. He considers work for one's ideal to be the best reward and happiness.

> *Verily I believed Thee O Mazda Ahura, to be the*
>   *Supreme Benevolent Providence,*
> *When the Good Mind came to me with*
>   *enlightenment,*
> *When first I received and became wise with Thy*
>   *words,*
> *And though the task be difficult, and hardship may*
>   *come my way,*
> *I shall proclaim Thy message, which Thou declarest*
>   *to be the best.*
> (Gathas: Yasna 43–11)

---

[21] The *Gathas: Yasnas* 32-15; 45-1; 48-5; 49-11.

The prophet covenants to spread the faith without concession and compromise.

> *Verily I believed Thee, O Mazda Ahura, to be the*
> *Supreme Benevolent Providence,*
> *When the Good Mind came to me and told me*
> *assuringly,*
> *That a reflective, contented mind is the best*
> *possession.*
> *Let not a leader compromise with, or propitiate evil–*
> *doers,*
> *For they treat the righteous as enemies.*
>
> (Gathas: Yasna 43–15)

The Younger Avesta informs us that Zoroaster married a girl by the name of *Hvovi* who became his first female disciple. Three of their six offspring were boys and three girls. *The Younger Avesta* gives the names of the children with the names of forty-one of the prophet's disciples.

At the age of seventy-seven, while praying in his oratory in Bactri (Balkh), the prophet was killed by Turbaratur, an enemy of the faith. Thus his martyrdom occurred forty-seven years after the revelation and at a time when Mazdaism had been already firmly established.

The Personality of the Prophet

From the content of the *Gathas* it is abundantly clear that Zoroaste was a natural man. He was an exceptionally wise and righteous person. He was an Ashu-one who had reached the apex of self-realization, perfection, and thenceforth immortality. He never had any claim to supernatural power or qualities. He was a mortal man, *Maretan,* who reached immortality by his appointment to prophethood. This is also reflected in the *Gathas*, where the Soul of Creation entreats God to appoint somebody from among the virtuous living mortal men, *Maravat*, as the saviour. *Asha* subscribes to that request. Both the Soul of Creation and *Asha* suggest that such a saviour should be the strongest of mortal men.

Thus to the Lord doth Asha, the Truth, reply:
"No guide is known who can shelter the world from
     woe,
None who knows what moves and works Thy lofty
     plans.
The most powerful of beings is he to whose help
     I shall go on an invocation."
                              (Gathas: Yasna 29–3)

Bewildered at the nomination of Zoroaster to prophethood, the Soul of Creation exclaimed that Zoroaster did not possess any worldly power. She expected a prince with a strong arm and an army to be chosen for the assignment. God tacitly alerted the Soul of Creation that in such a mission spiritual power and not worldly power is at issue. Instantaneously regretting her insolence, the Soul of Creation admitted that God knew best,[22] and requested God to grant the prophet-designate the mental strength and spiritual power to fulfill his mission. Thereupon God granted him the sweetness of speech as well. The prophet was a charismatic person with intelligence, the power of persuasion, and eloquence. Thus Zoroaster became the incarnation of perfection in this world and not, as is claimed by overzealous theosophists, an Ameshaspand.

It is significant that *Ahura Mazda* himself calls the prophet Zoroaster, meaning the Golden Light. Zoroaster consists of *Zaratha*, meaning golden, and *Ushtra* meaning light. According to one view the name given to the prophet at his birth was *Spitma*, after the clan or the house to which his father belonged, and Zoroaster was the name given to him after his enlightenment. A similar title, Buddha, was also given to Siddartha Gautama by his followers. According to a competing view, of the two components of Zoroaster's name, *Zarath* means yellow or old and *Ushtra* means camel, and the two words combined mean the owner of the yellow or old camel.

With the description of the prophet's personality given above, the miracles attributed to him in *The Younger Avesta* should not be taken in a literary sense. They should not be allowed to mar the true personality of a great prophet. Zoroaster was a natural man, a sage, a teacher, a philosopher, and a prophet and should be remembered and praised as such. There is no mystery in the

---

[22] The *Gathas*: *Yasna* 29-9, 10.

personality of the prophet. Zoroaster was not divinized in the *Gathas*. He was the heralder of a new religion and not only a reformer-a point which should be emphatically stressed. He believed in the Creator as the source of all goodness, in creation as an act of bounteousness, and in man as an agent of development and progress. He regarded creation as good and holy, and evil as aberration. He considered evil the product of man's wickedness. He declared moral dualism to be indispensable for the materialization of man's freedom of choice, and recognized the polarity between truth and falsehood inherent in it. He proclaimed the irreconcilability of Good and Evil; he recommended incessant battle against wickedness. He preached a life of hope, full of activity and enjoyment; he promised spiritual life after physical death. He condemned the traditional sacrificial ritual of slaughtering the ox and drinking the intoxicating stuff of the Homa plant. These were the teachings that made Zoroaster immortal.

The pre-Zoroastrian era was marked with widespread animism and various forms of nature worship. The solar cult was particularly important. Under that system the Athravans were primarily concerned with the proper celebration of rituals which were becoming more burdensome and costly to the populace. Instead of obsession with external purification rites and liturgy, Zoroaster stood for the observance of the essential tenets of the faith. He pleaded for direct and personal contact with God through wisdom, morality, and love rather than indirect and impersonal relationship through clergy-mediators; for selfless dedication to the advancement of the humanity rather than performances to please princes and priests. We see a similar populace movement at a later time, against Brahman, the priestly class in India; it resulted in the emergence of Jainism and Buddhism. The new ideas preached by Zoroaster appealed to both the intellectual elite and the pious masses.

The treatment of the clergy by the prophet Zoroaster is revealing. In the *Gathas*, Zoroaster calls himself *Zaota*, priest. So one expects a special mention in the *Gathas* of the priestly classes of that time–Athravan and Magi. Quite to the contrary, the prophet ignores them altogether. However, in the *Gathas* of Seven Chapters and in *The Younger Avesta*, the term Athravan, the fire priest of the Indo-Iranian era, reappears. The omission of Athravan in the *Gatbas* cannot be accidental. Either the prophet did not want their traditional duties to be continued or did not want Athravans as an exclusive priestly class to perform religious functions. The case is different with the Magis, the priestly class in western Iran, who opposed Zoroaster and his mission for many years. The word *Karapan* is used, probably in reference to them. The word *maga,* meaning "great," is employed in the *Gathas* of Seven Chapters in a generic sense and then only once. Though *The Younger Avesta* abounds in rituals, the silence of the *Gathas* on liturgy should not be taken as incidental. In search for an explanation, we note that in the *Gathas* Zoroaster reproaches the Karapans for their elaborately burdensome liturgy. The prophet worships God only with the simple rituals of "uplifted hands," "with deep and heartfelt reverence," and "with good thought, good word, and good deed."[23] These remarks cannot be taken lightly. The inference is that Zoroaster intends to convey the idea that one's duty as a Mazdaen is not discharged by performance of certain rituals and the mumbling of certain prayers. Deed and not word, intention and not spontaneity, sincerity and not pretension, count. Heartfelt conviction is a prominent feature of Mazdaism.

The rituals currently performed by Zoroastrians are the liturgy incorporated by the Magi in *The Younger Avesta.* On the salutary effect of the rituals, I may add a personal note here. Rituals that help mental concentration on a religion may be Justified; beyond that they are needless.

The Date and Birthplace of Zoroaster

In the absence of accurate information in the *Avesta* on the date and birthplace of the prophet Zoroaster, we must rely on the writings of historians.

Several points must be emphasized. First, the people of eastern Iran, where Zoroaster preached his religion, did not have a chronological notation computed from a given date as a basis.

---

[23] The *Gathas: Yasnas* 31-11, 32-14 (fermented juice of *Haoma),* 41-2, 3, 48-10. *Yasnas:* 1-11, 3-1, 37-13. In the *Gathas, Yasna* 28-1. Zoroaster prays, "O *Ahura Mazda,* with the uplifted hand and deep humility, I beseech you to grant me wisdom of the Good Mind, so that I perform all actions in harmony with *Asha.*" In *Yasna* 34-2: "By means of dedicated acts, dedicated words, and dedicated prayers."

Secondly, the genealogy of the prophet is not mentioned in the *Gathas*. Thirdly, the evidence on the matter is controversial. The Greeks who wrote about Zoroaster were far removed in time from him; the Sassanians wanted to make the establishment of the dynasty coincide with the millenium in the assumed Zoroastrian historical pattern.[24] Thus the antiquity of religion and manipulation of the time of the prophet for political reasons may provide an explanation for the divergence of opinion.

The Greek classical writers, quoting prominent historical personages like Aristotle, Hermodorus, and Xanthus (fifth century B.C.), date the prophet at six thousand years B.C. The Iranian writers of the Sassanian time, in an attempt both to assign the birth of Zoroaster to recorded history and to have its millenium coincide with the foundation of the Sassa.nian reign, post-dated it to the seventh century B.C. Thus they identified Vishtasp, during whose reign Zoroaster lived, with Hishtaspes, the father of Darius, the Achaemenian king. The two dates of the seventh millenium B.C. and the seventh century B.C. are labeled classical and traditional respectively.

As early as 500 A.D., Agathias, a Greek historian who was contemporaneous with the Pahlavi writers of the Sassanian period, wrote: "The time when Zoroaster flourished and gave his laws is not to be ascertained. The Persian nowadays simply say that he lived at the time of Hystaspes, but it is very doubtful, and the doubt cannot be solved whether this Hystaspes was the father of Darius, or another Hystaspes."[25] He continues: "At whatever time he may have lived, he was at all events their prophet.... After having changed the ancient form of worship, he introduced manifold and strange doctrines." Although in these statements Agathias was politically motivated and wanted to discredit Zoroastrianism and the Persian followers of that religion, his doubt as to the date of the prophet indicates that the traditional date did not enjoy the consensus of scholars even then.

The history of humanity shows that metallurgy developed as early as 7000 B.C. and that in western Asia the Iron Age started somewhat earlier than 1000 B.C. Iron is not mentioned in the *Gathas*, but metal or bronze, *Ayah*, is. Based on the reconstruction of material culture, can the appearance of this word be used

---

[24] Frye, 26-29.
[25] Martin, 11.

as an indication that Zoroastrianism was some time in the Bronze Age, that is, earlier than 1000 B.C.? The *Rig Veda* is dated as the eighteenth century B.C. Based on the reconstruction of the literary culture and religious beliefs, and bearing in mind that certain features of the Gathic language are more archaic than corresponding features in Vedic Sanskrit, can we date the birth of Zoroastrianism around that time? Contemporary Zoroastrianists are divided on this issue. While rejecting the classical Greek chronology, they, on the basis of tenuous linguistic and historical evidences, have suggested dates extending from the seventh[26] to the eleventh,[27] the fourteenth,[28] the fifteenth to the seventeenth,[29] and the eighteenth century B.C.[30] Recently the relics of a Zoroastrian temple are said to have been uncovered in Uzbekestan, Asia, and are dated by Soviet archeologists as 2000 B.C.[31] The earliest reference to Zoroastrianism in other holy scriptures is in the Old Testament[32] and the first historical account about the prophet is given by Herodotus.[33]

The birthplace of Zoroaster, according to the *Avesta*, is on the banks of the river Dareja[34] in Airyana Vaejah.[35] The homeland of Airyana Vaejah cannot be accurately located on the geographical map. If the term designated the land in which Iranian languages were spoken and the Iranian culture prevailed, on the present map of the world it would be an area covering parts of Transcaucasia, Central Asia, Northwest India, Mesopotamia, Afghanistan, and Iran. Some have mentioned Azarbayijan and Ragha (Rey) as the prophet's birthplace. Most scholars agree that he lived and taught in eastern Iran. He propagated his religion in Balkh and is said to have been killed in Balkh. The Gathic language belongs

---

[26] Jackson, 150-176.
[27] Sh. Shahbazi, "The Bulletin of the School of Oriental and African Studies," University of London, 1977, vol. XL, 7.
[28] Geldner, Encyclopeadia Britannica.
[29] Boyce, *Zoroastrians*: *TheirReligious Belief and Practices*, London: Routledge & Kegan Paul, 1979, 1.
[30] Zabih Behrooz.
[31] Ahmad Askarof, *Times of India*, Sept. 12, 1984.
[32] The Old Testament, Jeremiah xxxix, 3 (reference to Rab-Mag) and Ezekiel, viii, 16, 17.
[33] Herodotus, i, cxxxi and cxxxii.
[34] *Vendidad*, 19, 4.
[35] Frye, 29, 30.

to the languages of eastern Iran. Dareja is now identified as Araxes (Seyhoon in Persian) in Transoxiana; and the city of birth of the prophet was located near the northwestern frontier of Media.

Some scholars have suggested that the city of Ragha (presently Rey near Tehran) was the prophet's birthplace; and others have assumed it to have been "the seat of the prophet's ministry where he was both the spiritual and temporal chief [36] – an assertion that cannot be substantiated, particularly in view of the traditional city of his martyrdom, Balkh.

Prophets Before and After Zoroaster

The *Gathas* do not mention the name of any prophet before or after Zoroaster. According to the holy scriptures, Mazdaism revealed to Zoroaster is the best religion and the ideal way of life.[37]

The Younger Avesta, however, mentions the names of two persons in semi-prophetic positions: Gaya Maretan and Yima. Gaya Maretan, the primeval man, comes as the first mortal who heard the divine tenets. He was the first ruler of Iran, and the prototype of man (In Abrahamic religion "Adam" loosley corresponds to "Gaya Maretan"). The other person is Yima–Yama in Vedic–who was also king of Iran and the prototype of a good ruler. His reign was associated with justice, plentitude, and peace. He was alerted by God to the approach of three consecutive deadly cold winters that would destroy all the living things on earth. Yima constructed a cave, *vera,* into which he took the seeds of various plants, every kind of cattle, and the best human beings (In Abrahamic religion "Noah" loosley corresponds to "Yima"). According to Iranian mythology, Yima also ascended to the spiritual world and returned to earth. At one point God wanted Yima to be the prophet and to spread God's message. Considering the importance and difficulties of the mission, Yima pleaded inability and lack of confidence in himself to accept such a high mission. Toward the end of his reign, Yima became conceited and claimed divine power. As a result, God's grace left

---

[36] Dhalla, *History* 142.
[37] The Gathas: Yasna 44-10.

Yima and his kingship was lost to him. In the *Gathas* Yima is reproached as a sinner for allowing the slaughter of oxen for the pleasure of man.

The Younger Avesta also gives the name of Haoshangha, Gaya Maretan's successor, as the first lawgiver and the founder of the Para-Dhata dynasty. Para-Dhata means primitive law with a divine character. From all this we may conclude that before Zoroaster there were individuals who had visions, were inspired by the divine, and sporadically made laws, but Zoroaster was the first person to receive a prophetic ministry in the full sense of the term. Zoroaster was the first to receive a message and be commissioned to preach it.

The *Gathas,* in declaring Mazdaism the best religion forever, does not allude to prophets other than Zoroaster. However, it speaks of *Saoshyant.* In the form of *Soshyos, Saoshyant* reappears in *The Younger Avesta* as the chosen savior. *Saoshyant* has been used by scholars to mean *Messiah* or *Mahdi* in the Abrahamic religions.

Who is the *Saoshyant?* In the *Gathas, Saoshyant* is used in both singular and plural forms, though always in a generic sense, meaning the pious men who work for the improvement of the world. Thus all highly virtuous people like Gaya Maretan, Yima, before damnation, Haoshangha, Zoroaster and thousands of others may be considered *Saoshyant.* In *The Younger Avesta*, the situation changed and Soshyos, the Pahlavi rendering of *Saoshyant*, was employed for three specific persons who would come and help or complete the Great Renovation (Frash-Kreti = refreshment) of the world. All Soshyos will be sons born miraculously to Zoroaster. They will be from Zoroaster's seeds, through supernatural conception by three maids in three eras. They are not new prophets and do not preach new religions. They implement the law already revealed to Zoroaster. The *Gathas* remain the only divine code.

The *Gathas* present a God-centered creation, a Truth-centered community of man, and an order-based dynamism in the universe, in which God is the sublime source of ontological and axiological perfection. Zoroaster's God represents all positivity, constructiveness, and goodness. It negates all negativity, destruction, and evil. The *Gathas* stand out for their aphorisms; they do not address details. The law of *Asha* takes care of the details, and the medium of *Spenta Mainyu* sees that religious rules answer the creative needs of a changing society. All those principles in the *Gathas* make Mazdaism progressive and enable Zoroastrians to meet the exigencies of time without resort to any other way of life or religion. Practicing Zoroastrians believe in the revival and not in the renewal of Mazdaism.

Mazdaism is the great legacy left to humanity by Zoroaster. After several millenia, it is still a living faith and Zoroastrians everywhere are jealously protecting it against external incursions with the hope of faithfully passing it on to posterity. They believe in eternal life for those who act within the framework of *Asha* for the progress of humanity and the development of the world. That is *Ahura Mazda*'s will revealed through the prophet.

> *He, who following Truth, shall work for me,*
> *Zarathushtra,*
> *To bring us toward the Great Renovation, in*
> *accordance with Thy purpose,*
> *For him shall be all honor and content in this world,*
> *And a fitting state in the life beyond.*
> *As, verily, Thou hast revealed to me, O All-*
> *knowing Mazda!*
>
> (Gathas: Yasna 46–19)

To conclude, Zoroaster was a righteous mortal man who was appointed to prophethood. He preached a new religion, Mazdaism, revealed to him by *Ahura Mazda* in the holy book of the *Gathas*. His appointment to prophethood resulted as much from his righteousness, divine wisdom, and love for Truth as from *Ahura Mazda*'s benevolent choice. He was a philosopher–prophet. *Ahura Mazda's* message revealed to Zoroaster is contained in the *Gathas*, which is rational, practical, and universal. The *Gathas* are the spiritual and natural law for eternity. They contain prayers and the moral and civil code for behavior for mankind. Zoroastrians, wherever they may live, must observe the tenets of moral behavior laid down in the *Gathas* and join their prophet in a pledge to place their trust in *Ahura Mazda* and by means of dedicated acts, dedicated words, and dedicated prayers performed in his name, gain holy wisdom (*Vohu Mana*), righteousness-with-justice (*Asha*), moral courage (*Khshatra*) to serve others with tranquility and love (*Armaity*); achieve self-realization and perfection (*Haurvatat*); and finally attain immortality (*Ameretat*) and everlasting happiness (*Ushta*) in unison with the Eternal Reality-the Essence of Goodness.

III

ASHA

The Pinciple of Eternal Law and justice–God's Will

Mazda, where are the devotees who know
  of Vohu man? In trouble and distress,
This knowledge of their Herritage Divine
  Brings Freedom to their intellect and mind;
None else than Ye e'er will we recognize;
  So shelter us under Eternal Law.
  (Gathas: Yasna 34–7)

History

Asha denotes law, righteousness, and justice. To do justice means to do the right thing, and no act can be right unless it is congruous with the law of *Asha.* The law of *Asha* requires self-less service with love and dedication for the preservation, development, and refreshment of the world.

Asha is the second attribute –next to Good Mind (*Vohu Mana*)– and yet the most frequently mentioned attribute of God in the *Gathas*. It is the very foundation of Mazdaism. Truth and Good Mind are intimately associated; perhaps the Good Mind is more active "as the medium through which God prefers to reveal Himself."[1] In the *Gathas, Ahura Mazda* is considered Father of *Asha*, good mind, and god's other attributes. God, Good Mind,

---

[1] W. B. Henning, *Zoroaster,* New York: Oxford, 1951, 46.

and Truth are referred to by scholars as "the divine Triad."[2] No
exact counterpart of the word *Asha* exists in English.

Asha connotes the eternal, immutable and causative law that
governs the universe. It is the divine law that regulates both the
spiritual and the corporeal worlds. In Zoroastrianism the natural
and divine laws are the same. *Asha* also signifies the ideal moral,
social, and natural order that should prevail in the world. It denotes the ideal truth.

Ahura Mazda conceived the universe in his mind (*Vohu
Mana*),[3] fashioned it in his conscience (*Daēnā*),[4] manifested it
through his creativity (*Spenta Mainyu*)[5] and set it in motion in
accordance with his eternal law (*Asha*).[6] God is *Asha* and *Asha*
represents God's Will. The *Gathas* declare that *Asha* is of one
will with *Ahura Mazda*.[7]

The existence of an eternal law and order in one form or another is deeply rooted in Indo-Iranian culture. *Asha* can be traced
to the pre-Zoroastrian era. In old Persian inscriptions it is *Arta*.
Its Vedic equivalent is *Rta*. *Ahura Mazda* entrusted his worthiest
friend and coworker, Zoroaster, with the eternal law of *Asha* and
commissioned him to pass it on to mankind. Zoroaster, even before revelation, was acting according to *Asha*,[8] so he can be considered the embodiment of *Asha* in this world.

In Eastern religious traditions, another concept related to the
"ethical and social law" exists which is designated *dharma* (Sanskrit) in Hinduism and *Dhamma* (Pali) in Buddhism. Dharma
stems from the word *dhr*, meaning "upholding." *Dharma* is the
moral and social foundation of Hinduism and Buddhism, as *Asha*

---

[2] Carter, 53.

[3] The *Gathas*; *Yasna* 44 4, 5, 7 (Sublime Mind [is] the first attribute and
the first creation of *Ahura Mazda*; *Ahura Mazda* created and sustained
the universe through Wisdom; *Asha* and other attributes of *Ahura
Mazda* were emanated through his sublime mind.)

[4] The *Gathas*; *Yasna* 44-10 (*Abura Mazda* shaped and promoted life
through his *Daena*; *Daena* is the only religion that makes man happy.)

[5] *The Gathas*; *Yasna* 47-3 (*Abura Mazda* created the joy-giving earth);
Yasnas 51-7; 47-1, 2, 3 (*Abura Mazda* created earth, plants, water, and
so forth, through *Spenta Mainyu*.)

[6] The *Gathas*; *Yasna* 31-7, 8; 47-3 (*Asha* emanated from good mind.)

[7] The *Gathas*; *Yasna* 28-8 (*Ahura Mazda, Vohu Mana and Asha* are
inseparable and are of one will.)

[8] The *Gathas*; *Yasnas* 29-8, 28-6.

is the divine and natural foundation of Mazdaism. Both signify righteousness and good ethics.

The law of *Asha* is as changeless as God himself. It rules the process of gradual renovation of the world. It is changeless, although it regulates changes in the world and determines world dynamism. It represents the causative law: the relation between an individual's actions and their consequences. Karma in Buddhism stands for the same causative law. In Mazdaism, it is one's action that determines the direction of his life and his fortune. An individual is free to choose his course of action and set the accrual of certain consequences in motion. The consequences of each action are predetermined, but the choice of action for man is not. Thus the fate of man is not preordained. Once the choice is made and the direction of life is set, the consequences of an individual's thoughts, words, and deeds will follow in accordance with the law of *Asha*. This is God's will and God's justice.

Asha denotes *righteousness*. It constitutes the yardstick for the determination of the rightness and wrongness of acts. It sets normative ethics. It lays down the standards that apply to all people at all times. It represents *absolute as well as the ideal values*. In general terms, the *Gathas* state the essentials and formulate the behavioral standards for the benefit of human beings who are expected to conform truthfully to the general guidelines in which process good and holy reasoning must be applied. Relativism is contrary to the Gathic morality. The basic assumption is that right deeds produce benefits for the individual author of the action as well as for the society. Conversely, evil deeds harm both the agent of the evil acts and the society. The accrual of the benefits to the agent of the act is automatic. Therefore the question of egoism and utilitarianism entertained in moral philosophy does not arise.[9] In Mazdaism the basic principle is that the real benefits of good acts for individuals and society match. The perceived benefits may be different. *Asha* determines the real and not the perceived advantages. Mazdaism believes in the universal criteria that apply to all situations. According to the law of *Asha*, rightness of deeds are grounded both in Good Mind (*Vohu Mana*) and in *Asha* (Righteousness and Justice). Righteous deeds should be performed Selflessly and with Loyalty and

---

[9] When both the individual and group interests are regulated by *Asha*, no conflict can appear.

Love (*Armaity*), for rightness of acts cause the mind and conscience to operate in unison.

> *That I the* better way *might choose, reveal,*
> *what in accord with* Truth *Thou has ordained;*
> *Reveal to me through* Love, *through* Vohu Mana,
> *that I might be uplifted and be sure,*
> *Whatever comes at Thy command is best,*
> *for me, whatever reward or otherwise.*
> (Gathas: Yasna 31–5)

The right act should be chosen through good reasoning and in
accordance with *Asha*. This enables human beings, with God-
given faculties, to apply the absolute principle of *Ash* to changing circumstances in a manner to achieve ideal justice. The in-
compatibility of relativism is thus being avoided. The choice
should be made with love and a sense of duty. Dutifulness is an
essential part of Zoroastrian morality.

> *Such are the saviors of the earth,*
> *Who, inspired by the Good Mind, cause betterment,*
> *By actions in tune with the laws of Truth and justice.*
> *They are indeed appointed by Thee to dispel*
> *violence, O Mazda!*
> (Gathas: Yasna 48-12)

The moral standards are those set by God's attributes in which
process the Holy Spirit, Good Mind, Love, and Righteousness
(justice) participate. These standards, therefore, cannot be egois-
tic, because they aim at the eradication of hatred and self-
interest.

Thus in Zoroastrian metaethics, the determination of rightness and wrongness takes place by weighing them against several principles, *Asha and Vohu Mana* remaining the yardsticks.
To make it more practical, Zoroaster has formulated the often-
quoted maxims of *Good Thought, Good Word* and *Good Deed.*
The three maxims describe the principle of *Asha* in action.
Ahura Mazda has bestowed faculties on man whereby he can
discern between the rightness and wrongness of his actions and
make considered decisions. The law of *Asha* ensures that happy
consequences flow from good acts. *Asha* also guarantees the final victory of righteousness over falsehood that evokes God's

omnipotence. Righteousness is best of all that is good and is the radiant goal of life on earth. One must live righteously and for the sake of righteousness alone. Worldly rewards should not be the motivation. Duty for the sake of duty constitutes selfless service.[10]

The realization process of Good's triumph over Evil is gradual and not abrupt.[11] A dutiful human being, as a friend and co-worker of God, endeavors to propagate virtue and righteousness and to eradicate falsehood and wickedness. His intention should be the advancement of the world toward victory and the final establishment of the kingdom of God on earth.[12]

A Zoroastrian does not do his duty if he only keeps himself away from wickedness-active, not a passive righteousness is required. A Zoroastrian is duty-bound to do his best to guide and save others from being drowned in sin and falsity. This is one aspect of Zoroastrian positivity, translated into a good life, striving for the world's refreshment.

Although the *Gathas* generally state only the principles, later the *Avesta* defines in detail the character of certain types of behavior. Certain norms of conduct are highly recommended and a number of demeanors are strictly forbidden. One totally abhorred behavior throughout the *Avesta* is wrath, *Aeshma.* It is considered an outrageously vile act leading to violence that harms both the agent of the act and the society. The *Gathas* state that wrath hinders sound judgment and righteous deeds; it creates hatred in the heart and gossip on the tongue. An angry person cannot love the Truth and he becomes a monster in human form.[13] This mon-

---

[10] The *Gathas*; *Yasna* 48-12 (Everybody must follow the call of duty by good thought, and in all deeds one must be inspired by righteousness. *Yasna* 27-14. (When one lives righteously for the sake of the highest righteousness alone, one attains happiness.)

[11] The *Gathas*; *Yasnas* 43-12, 16; 51-6, 7, 13. The process is gradual and the triumph does not come abruptly through the act of the last saviour. This belief has been preserved in Zoroastrian tradition. *See Dinkard*, vol. 47, 7, 10.9, 114 and *Bundahishn*, 30-1. By that time men do not cat meat and live only on water and vegetables; no injustice and no disharmony exist in the world. The Saviours comes to give the final touch to this great event.

[12] The *Gathas*; *Yasna* 34-15.

[13] The *Gathas*; *Yasnas* 46-8; 48-7; 49-4.

ster, the evil-doer, is prompted by an evil mentality that causes wrath and is produced by wrath.

A norm of conduct highly recommended is *dutifulness* or *selfless service.* Duty should be done for the sake of duty and not in expectation of reward. Performed selflessly and conscientiously, the reward would accrue through the operation of law.[14] The good of mankind as a whole and the progress of the world should be the main objective in man's activities.[15] Righteousness is the duty assigned to man by God's will. Honesty, *Arsh Mangha*, and fulfillment of the promise, *Mithra*, are emphasized. Fulfillment of promises and honoring of contracts relates to all dealings including commercial transactions. *Mithra* chastizes those who commit breach of contract. In contrast, falsehood, *Drauga*, lies, *Druj*, and violence, *Renen*, are emphatically censured. Mercy and compassion, *Marezehdika*, towards deserving people and charity, *Rata*, to the needy are also strongly recommended. The honesty and charity for which the Zoroastrians are renowned throughout the world stems from their religious beliefs and traditions.

The conceptualization of the moral norms set out in the *Gathas* helps foster a better understanding of the major features of the Gathic doctrine of *Asha.*

The Liberty of Man

Man's liberty is the most precious of God's bounties. It is a component of divine law; it is the natural right of every human being. The concept of slavery, even in its mildest form, is alien and repugnant to Zoroastrianism. Man's liberty is so inalienable that God does not curtail man's freedom of action even with regard to man's choice of religion. An individual, if he so prefers, can opt for wickedness. God in his justice (*Asha*), however, warns man in advance of the consequences of evil actions.[16] In his first sermon the prophet thus preaches:

> *Hearken with your ears to these best counsels:*
> *Gaze at the beams of fire and contemplate*

---

[14] The *Gathas*; *Yasnas* 43-9; 32-6; 31-1, 2; 32-6; 44-15. Reward comes through the operation of law.

[15] The *Gathas*; *Yasna* 31-4, 16; 43-2; 44-8; 46-10; 48-5, 7; 49-9.

[16] The *Gathas*; *Yasnas* 47-6; 48-2, 3, 4; 49-3. *Ahura Mazda* in his justice has warned man not to do evil.

> *with your best judgment:*
> Let each man/woman choose his/her creed, *with that* freedom
>   of choice *which each must have at great events;*
> *O ye, awake of these my announcements!*
>   (Gathas: Yasna 30–2)

Zoroastrianism is the religion of free will *par excellence*. This freedom is prescribed for all man's transactions and commitments. Few prophets have invited their audience to weigh the tenets of the faith with reasoning, good mind, and conscience.

> *Hearken unto me, O ye who come from near and*
>   *from far!*
> *Listen to me, as I speak forth now,*
> *Ponder over these teachings with care and clear*
>   *thought.*
> *Never shall the False Teacher destroy existence a*
>   *second time,*
> *For his tongue stands mute, his creed stands*
>   *exposed.*
>   (Gathas: Yasna 45–1)

The prophet also emphasizes the importance of good knowledge and the necessary insight into religion before making any decision.

> *Before the* struggle *in my* mind *begins,*
> *Tell me,* Ahura, all that I should know,
> *Give me the* knowledge *and assurance, Lord,*
> *That Righteousness shall overcome Untruth;*
> *Such is* Thy plan - *the Final Shape of Life.*
>   (Gathas: Yasna 48-1)

The right of liberty is also reflected in the Zoroastrian concept of the God-man relationship. Unlike Islam, in which man is Abd, or the slave of God, and unlike Christianity, in which man is God's child, Zoroastrianism considers man as the coworker and friend of God. Hence neither the owner's right, nor paternal authority, can contain man's freedom of choice. The restraining force comes from the individual's moral convictions, conscience (*Daena*), and good mind (*Vohu Mana*). Likewise, the Christian idea of original sin is repugnant to Zoroastrians.

Actions originate in mind. Holy reasoning creates *will*, which is expressed by *words* and put into *deeds*. The sequence of the practical moral maxims of good thought, good word, and good deed reflects the pre-eminence of thought. In Mazdaism the *Will* is the source of moral behavior.

Ahura Mazda does not want his coworkers to accept things blindly or under compulsion. At all times all the truth should be learned and preached. Under no circumstances should one lie or conceal the truth. Free will and religious awareness are essential elements for a credible conversion to the faith, elements that make conversion a matter of conviction and acceptance. Formal declaration without intent has no validity and this differentiates Mazdaism from those religions that rely only on the formal acknowledgment of faith, even if under compulsion.

Nature and the Environment

Any act ravaging nature is forbidden. That is why Zoroastrianism is called the first ecological religion.[17] Protection of the environment is an aspect of *Asha*. Defilement of the soil, water, air, and fire in any form or degree is considered a transgression of nature and of the law of *Asha*. This protective attitude toward nature originates in the Gathic treatment of life and the material world. A vast difference exists between those religions that view matter as an evil substance and the body as a prison for the soul, and Zoroastrianism, which treats matter and life as benefactions from God and, as such, adorable. Life and matter, if put to good use, are loving and divinely vouchsafed. *Ahura Mazda* is the architect of both celestial and terrestrial worlds. His creations, without any exception, are good. This joy-producing world is being sustained by *Ahura Mazda*, and human beings as his coworkers must act wisely and gratefully in the preservation of the world. God's love and wisdom protect the earth and establish peace and progress on it.

God has given all this bounty out of love for mankind and other creatures. He has proclaimed himself the benefactor of the world. As his coworkers, friends and as beneficiaries of his gifts, man must not be destructive to nature. On the contrary, man

---

[17] Nature, in Zoroastrianism, is not only a proof of the existence of God (*Gathas: Yasna* 44-3, 4, 5, 6); it is created to give joy to man (*Gathas: Yasna* 38-1). The all-pervading *Atar barezi-savah* that penetrates the earth is praised in *Yasna* 17-11.

must exert all efforts to develop and advance the world. The world should progress and achieve perfection through man's achievements, with the help of *Asha* and *Vohu Mana*. This belief explains Zoroaster's immense veneration of all the components and elements of nature and indeed for all God's creatures. At times this attitude has been misinterpreted by unwary observers as polytheistic. A Zoroastrian extolls nature as an acknowledgment of the greatness and glory of God; he preserves it as a token of gratitude.

The *Avesta* is replete with praise for the sanctity of natural elements. In the "Prayers in Respect of Four Directions" or "*Namac i char Nem,*" a Zoroastrian bows to the four directions the world over, implying that he has respect for nature and thereby testifies to the omnipotence of *Ahura Mazda.* There are special adorations for various aspects and components of the universe, including the sun, stars, earth, water, soil, air, and fire. In Zoroastrian prayers the intrinsic purity and usefulness of those planets and elements are reaffirmed and eulogized, while their contamination is condemned. The tower of silence was introduced as a method of disposal of the dead corpse in order to avoid the defilement of soil and the waste of useful crop-growing earth. Little objective study of the method has been made by non-Zoroastrians, and yet many sensational reports have been written. An objective investigation would show that the end result of disposing of the corpse in the tower of silence and by cremation is the same.

By offering homage to water, fire, earth, air, and other natural elements in his prayers, a Zoroastrian acknowledges the importance of keeping nature free from pollution. The natural elements are essential for existence and progress: they are sources of energy and indispensable for the continuation of life. Human beings are acting as trustees for nature in this world; anybody who violates that trust encroaches upon the law of *Asha* and will encounter unhappiness in life.

In an attempt to enhance popular consciousness of the natural elements (short of reintroducing pre-Zoroastrian polytheism), Zoroastrian sages introduced the concept of *Yazatas*, the Adorable Ones, who represent the natural elements and are also their guardians; and made them praiseworthy. For instance, in the framework of the Adorables, Anahita represents water and is also the guardian of water, and Atar represents fire and at the same time is the genius of fire. Anahita bestows fertility on women, purifies the male's seeds, purges the woman's wombs, facilitates the child's birth, and provides timely milk in mothers' breasts. Likewise, Atar is the bestower of well-being, abundance, wisdom, comprehension, and a host of other boons on man. The metaphors and symbolism employed in the concept of *Yazatas* are most graceful and impressive. They nurture love and the care of nature in the hearts and minds of multitudes of people.

Human Rights

Zoroastrianism is the first religion that has taken a doctrinal and political stand on the subject of human rights and has condemned the limitation or curtailment of those rights under any pretext.[18]

Although it is a modern legal coinage not used in religious literatures of the past, the concept of human rights as a system of values and ideas is ingrained in Mazdaism. In Zoroastrianism the idea of human rights stems from the principle that man is created to be a coworker with God and as such ought to try to emulate the master of the craft. Being only a good creator, God has created the universe and man as essentially good. The Soul of Creation's complaints about rape, violence and passion; King Yima's fall from power due to his vanity and nonobservance of the law; the prophet's insistence on freedom of choice in acceptance of a faith; Zoroaster's advice to his daughter to respond to the call of wisdom and love in her choice of a bridegroom; the recognition of the equality of men and women in all respects; the condemnation of autocratic and unjust rule and the recommendation to the faithful not to submit to oppressive rulers-all these demonstrate the values of human rights in Zoroastrianism. The Mazdaen notion of human rights is the natural extension of the two doctrines of the goodness of God and the function of man as God's coworker. By sharing God's attributes, man has "God's stamp"; therefore man must do good. Serving others with altruistic dedication is a component of being good. *Asha* requires justice in attitude and behavior, and a just man must behave accordingly. Anger and revenge, oppression and exploitation, extortion and

---

[18] John R. Hinnels, "The Theory and Practice of Human Rights in Zoroastrianism," paper presented to the Fourth World Zoroastrian Congress, Bombay, 1985.

trespassing, are not godly qualities and man should avoid them. Anger and violence are next to lying in offensiveness. Physical assault and mental torture are reprehensible acts, whether committed by individuals or by governments; they are strictly forbidden.

There is a great difference between those religions that consider mortal life as a period of bondage and Zoroastrianism, which views life as sacrosanct. In Zoroastrianism the body is not diabolical and matter is not evil. Zoroastrianism views soul and body "as a harmonious whole, the unity of which temporarily is disrupted by death, but fully restored and glorified at the final Renovation."[19] Unlike the situation in the dualism of good and evil, body and soul are not mutually hostile in Zoroastrianism, although they remain different entities. Body and soul are complementary to each other. Therefore, Zoroastrians are opposed to any form of asceticism. In Mazdaism the integrity of the human body, *Tanu*, and the human soul, *Urvan*, are valued; physical or mental assaults are repugnant acts. The religious emphasis on righteousness, order, and a harmonious life necessitates a full observance of justice and equity. This emphasis constitutes the general principle that no one should suffer mental or physical abuse from others.

> *In accordance with the Primeval Laws of this*
>   *existence,*
> *The Ratu (Judge) shall deal perfect justice to all;*
> *To the good who chose the Truth,*
> *To the evil who chose Falsehood,*
> *And to those in whom good and evil are mixed.*
>   (Gathas: Yasna 33–1)

This stanza demonstrates an important human issue: fair and human treatment of culprits, enemies, and foes. It recommends that men should act in full agreement with the principle of justice, which contains the fundamental laws of life. This stanza distinguishes three groups of people: the True people (*Ashvan*), the False (*Dregvan*), and those who have mixed records of truth and falsehood. According to various Gathic passages, even the False should be treated justly: all their deeds should be accounted for.

---

[19] Zaehner, *The Teachings*, 54.

The commitment to equality of human beings, irrespective of ethnic origin and sex, is evident in the *Gathas*. The *Gathas* give equal praise to *Fryana* of the Turanian ethnic group and to Maidyomah, the prophet's nephew, and to Jamaspa of the Hvogva tribe. The privileges of people are commensurate with their righteousness and not with their ethnic affiliation.

The equality of males and females is unreservedly admitted. The particular attention given to the equality of sexes in Zoroastrianism is not matched by any other religion. In all his sermons the prophet gives recognition to man, *Na*, and woman, *Nairi*, by addressing them separately and on equal footing. He gives both men and women complete freedom in the choice of creed and marriage. In a sermon addressed to his daughter Pouru-Chista, Zoroaster teaches young men and women to consult with their inner self–with their perfect wisdom and love (*Armaity*)–before entering into the uniting bond of marriage.[20] Overwhelmed with the equality of the sexes to the holy scriptures, Zoroastrian sages extended the Gathic principle of the equality of the sexes to the attributes of God. In *The Younger Avesta* the names of the three attributes retain their Gathic female gender, and three other names reflect the male gender. Philologically the nonfemale words had a neutral gender in the *Gathas*.[21]

No caste system or class privilege is recognized in the *Gathas*. Mazdaism rose against the caste system prevalent in Indo-Iranian societies. In the *Gathas* the prophet reprimands the two classes of Karapans and Kavis; he avoids any allusion to Athravan and Magis as a class lest that would be interpreted as an implied recognition of hereditary privilege in the priesthood.

The class system of the Sassanian era, of priests, warriors, husbandmen, and artisans had its roots in pre-Gathic Iranian society, probably reintroduced by the Magi. The marriage between the church and state in the Sassanian period tried to legitimize the caste system. The comparatively rapid decline of Zoroastrianism after the Arab-Islam conquest was partly due to the erroneous identification of Zoroastrianism with the oppressive acts and class discrimination of the Sassanian era.

The *Gathas* recognize only a vertical social structure based on *Nmana* (family), *Vis* (clan or village), *Zantu* (tribe or city),

---

[20] The *Gathas*; *Yasnas* 53-5, 6, 7, 8; 51-17.
[21] Dhalla, *History*, 49.

and *Dahyu* (country). The word *slavery* is nonexistent in the *Gathas*. The three groups–*Xvaetu, Airyaman, Verezena*–mentioned in the *Gathas* are not associated with any privilege. Dhalla thought they refer to "Immediate disciples, the nobility and the working class."[22] Taraporewala defined them as "three grades of Zoroaster's disciples," and translated the words into "self-reliant, coworker, and friend."[23]

Religion and Polity

All religions stand for justice; all governments have a claim on it. Yet its contents and connotations in various religions and polities differ.

The following characteristics are discernable in the Zoroastrian concept of Justice: (1) The divine nature of justice is the fundamental principle. Consequently no man-made law should negate the divine law, as propounded in the *Gathas*. The Gathic doctrines are enunciated in general terms; the details are left to man to legislate within the Gathic legal framework in the light of society's stage of progress; (2) Religion and polity–or the church and state–are twins.[24] They operate hand in hand; though one should not manipulate the other for its own advantage. The harmonious cooperation of the twins does not require the identity or marriage of church and state;[25] and (3) Strict observance of the positive law is enacted in accord with the principle of *asha*. Greek historians have given accounts of the strict observance of justice during the Medes and the Achaemenians. "The laws of Medes and Persians are immutable," was the adage; it meant the law, irrespective of a perpetrator's social status, would be applied. The strict application of the law in Mazdaism, amounting to equity, should be considered in the context of the underlying principle of reasonableness and love running through the religion.

Mazdaism denounces autocratic and unjust rulers. In several passages, the *Gathas* instruct the *Ashvan* against submission to the rule of unjust and ruthless governors. The *Ashvan* are directed to support only the righteous rulers who, being guided by

---

[22] Ibid. 74.

[23] Iraj Taraporewala, footnote to *Yasna* 32-1.

[24] Zaehner, *The Dawn,* 297.

[25] During Sassanian, the church was powerful. However in the gathas the church as an institution, has no relevance.

Ahura Mazda's good wisdom and love, would dedicate their lives to the realization of Truth. The *Ashvan* must unite in their opposition to despotic rulers, and in their support of benevolent rulers.[26]

> *A righteous government is of all the most to be*
>   *wished for,*
> *Bearing of blessing and good fortune in the highest.*
> *Guided by the law of Truth, supported by*
>   *dedication and zeal,*
> *It blossoms into the Best of Order, a Kingdom of*
>   *Heaven!*
> *To effect this I shall work now and ever more.*
>   (Gathas: Yasna 51–1)

An Active and Constructive Life

This is an important component of the principle of *Asha*. The Gathic moral code consists of recommended actions and abstentions. Idleness is a feature of evil and is censured. Divine wisdom, righteousness, and moral courage pertain to those who choose to be active.

> *The best work of this Bountiful spirit, he fulfils*
> *Endowed with the Good Mind, speaks word of*
>   *wisdom,*
> *Works with his hands as prompted by active*
>   *Benevolence,*
> *Inspired by the insight that Thou, O Mazda, art the*
>   *Father of Truth.*
>   (Gathas: Yasna 47–2)

The prophet teaches his disciples to be unceasingly active.

> *O wise Jamaspa Hvogva, I have taught,*
> *That action, not inaction, higher stands,*
> *Obeying, then, His Will, worship through deeds;*
> *The Great Lord and Guardian of the Worlds,*
> *Through His Eternal Law discriminates,*
> *who are the truly Wise and who Unwise.*
>   (Gathas: Yasna 46–17)

---

[26] The *Gathas*; *Yasnas* 48-5, 53-4.

To be active is to cleanse the heart from wrath and wickedness, to preach truth, to direct others to become virtuous and to unite with other righteous people in endeavors for the advancement of the world. To be active implies making the right choice. The principle of right choice also applies to the election of righteous people as social and political leaders. The *Gathas* direct that in worldly affairs, when one has to choose a leader from among mortals, one must choose a leader who is true to *Asha,* to love for wisdom, to dedicated service to mankind, and to an insatiable desire for the propagation of truth, the exercise of justice, and the refreshment of the world.[27] Monasticism, celibacy, asceticism, and self-mortification have no place in Mazdaism. The function of *Asha* is to preserve life and vitality in this world and to give man an opportunity to enhance his moral apprehension.[28] The aim of life is happiness, *Ushta.*[29] The imperatives of happiness are the establishment of harmony and unity, first, between one's body, *Tanu,* and soul, *Urvan*; and secondly, between the individual and the society. Harmony has a dual aspect: inwardly within oneself and outwardly within the society. While recognizing the individuality of man, particularly through freedom of choice, *Avesta* puts a great emphasis on the man's social identity.

Man's activities should be for the cause of righteousness. *Life is the battlefield between Good and Evil,* and human beings should act as warriors for Good. Those who work for the progress and perfection of the world through the guidance of their conscience, *Daena,* and in harmony with the law of *Asha,* earn an everlasting *Ushta.* Those who commit falsehood, or hinder the activities of *Ashvan,* or remain insensitive to the attempts of *Dregvan,* will suffer a miserable life. The *Gathas* call on *Ashvan*

---

[27] John Waterhouse, *Zoroastrianism,* London: The Epworth Press, 79.

[28] The *Gathas*; *Yasna* 43-1; Zaehner, The Dawn, 156: "The order of *Ahura Mazda* is based on rectitude, peace, and prosperity, and it is his intention for man that he should prosper and be happy in a peaceful society."

[29] The vertical structure of the Iranian society is reflected in the Five Gahs, which are cited with other prayers in the relevant time. *Nmana, Vis, Zantu, Dahyu,* and *Khshatra.* *Khvateu* (family or khanevadeh in Farsi) lived in *Nmana* (house), *Varezana* (clan) lived in the *Vis* (settlement) and *Airyaman* (People with mutual and common bonds of rights and duties) lived in *Zantu* (territory); *Gathas: Yasnas* 53-7; 51-11, 15.

to pursue a continuous and uncompromising fight against evil, even at the risk of endangering their own lives. The fight must always start in the individual's mind with an attempt to discard evil mentality. Hatred, wrath, and the use of physical force must be avoided. Correction of others should be done only through preaching, guidance, and setting good examples. One should never hide his religion and truth even if his life be threatened.

One's activities should harm neither the quality of one's spiritual and physical life nor that of the society in which one lives. The importance of one's duties to the community and society is reflected in the five-times-daily prayers of Zoroastrians. A follower of the faith invokes the blessings of *Ahura Mazda*; at dawn for the righteous head and the members of the household, *Nman*; in the morning for the righteous head and members of the village, *Savan*; at noon for the righteous leader and the residents of the city, *Zantum*; in the evening for the righteous leader and people of the country, *Dakhy*; and at night for the righteous leader, *Rathu*, of the religion of Righteousness and all Righteous and just people, *Ashvan*, who tread the path of *Asha*.[30] *Ushta* goes to whoever joins the *Brotherhood of Ashvan*.

> *When you come within our* Brotherhood,
> *You will understand the merits of True Life,*
> *Of wedded bliss in its devoted zeal,*
> *Whether you strive for this life or the next;*
> *But should you choose to leave the Brotherhood,*
> *Deluded by the Spiiit of Untruth,*
> *Then grief and words of woe shall be your end.*
> (Gathas: Yasna 52–7)

A Mazdayasnan believes that no conflict between personal and societal interests will be encountered by those who act in accordance with the law of *Asha*. But should such a variance present itself, a Mazdayasnan should always give precedence to society's interests. Thus Zoroastrian ethics are utilitarian and not egotistic.

The concept of *Asha* signifies the realization of justice without fear or favor, without mediation or discrimination, and without any regard to one's social standing. In Zoroastrianism no one can mediate to change the consequences of the law of *Asha*.

---

[30] Dhalla, *History*, 56.

Asha is an ongoing process; in it justice and righteousness merge and form the law. As justice, *Asha* manifests the law of consequences, action-reaction and cause-effect. An individual who chooses the path of *Asha, Ashahe Panteo*, will attain Eternal Light and, in the end, Immortality.

Zoroaster conceives right (*Asha*) as might (*Khshatra*); the temporal might is not right unless gained and employed for the cause of justice.[31] He says that while the temporal rulers may appear powerful, the real might lies with the virtuous man due to his wisdom and *Asha*.

> *The Highest and the Best shall come to* him,
> *who learning Wisdom, shall my message spread,*
> *The Holy Word, which the perfection leads,*
> *And the Eternal Life-the* word of Truth,
> *Mazda's own Might, shall* come to him *for this,*
> *And grow* through Wisdom from *strength to strength.*
>   (Gathas: Yasna 31–6)

Individuals can, according to the *Gathas*, choose to be just or unjust; however the *Gathas* caution that justice is more rewarding. An unjust person may attain an illusionary, initial success; in the end, through the operation of the eternal law of justice, he will prove a failure.[32] The unjust distort things and attempt to disturb the scheme of life. They apply all their talents to disrupt the operation of the law of *Asha*, but Wisdom and Truth working in unison will bring about justice.[33]

Spiritual Militancy and Physical Self-Restraint

While abhorring physical violence, Zoroastrianism advocates mental militancy. The *Gathas* teach us that good and evil are irreconcilable; the false tries to destroy the true; and truthful people should not collaborate with liars. The false teacher distorts the scriptures, and thereby distorts the scheme of life.[34] The righteous must fight evil. The struggle must originate within the self and then be extended to other people.

---

[31] The *Gathas*; *Yasna* 31-13, 14, 15.

[32] The *Gathas*; *Yasnas* 32-6; 51-13; 53-8.

[33] The *Gatbas*; *Yasna* 31-12, 15, 18.

[34] This inference is from the *Gathas*: *Yasna* 31-18, where it is said that the wicked destroys his household, city, country, and the world.

So let no one give heed to Teachers False,
Nor to their words and teachings lend ear;
Because the home, the town, the province, too
And e'en the country, would the False One hurl
Down to the world of torment and of death;
Resist *them with your* Inner Spirit's sword.
(Gathas: Yasna 31–18)

This stanza also gives us the five levels of authority and gov-
ernance in society. After defeating the evil mind within oneself,
everyone must eliminate evil thoughts in one's household, village, tribe (or city), province, country, and ultimately the whole
world.[35]

Asha *is Mean*

In later Zoroastrian tradition, *Asha* is identified with the
mean. Any material and spiritual deficiency is considered contrary to divine law and order. "In the material order, the mean
manifests itself as health; excess and deficiency as sickness; in
the spiritual order, the mean consists in virtue, while excess and
deficiency appear as the vices."[36] The mean is also a feature of,
or even the essence of, *Khratu* or intelligence; thus the mean in
the younger tradition becomes a constant companion of Wisdom,
as *Asha* in the Gathic tradition was the permanent associate of
Vohu Mana.

Thus, mean becomes central to physical and moral order.
Mean becomes truth and justice. Virtue is the mean, and excess
in either direction is a vice. Courage is a virtue; boldness and
fear are vices. Moderation is a virtue; all moderate acts originate
in wisdom and truth and pertain to Ultimate Reality.

To conclude, *Asha* represents the Universal Divine Order. It
regulates both the physical and the spiritual worlds. It signifies
the cosmic and the social order; it is the essence of order. *Asha* is
the right path; it is the religion. Practicing Zoroastrians regard
Asha as God's will. Zoroaster's teachings are against fatalism.
Every person is free to make his or her choice. Once the choice
is made, the consequences flow from the law of *Asha. Asha* is
justice and righteousness. *Asha* is the Ideal Truth. Excesses are
contrary to the law of *Asha. Asha* stands for liberty and the

---

[35] Zaehner, *The Dawn* 286.
[36] Safa, 302.

equality of man, for respect and the protection of nature and the environment, for truth and moderation, and for a constructive and productive life. Zoroastrians, in their daily prayers, acknowledge that there is only one right path and that is the path of *Asha*; all other paths lead to falsehood.

IV

GOOD AND EVIL

Principles of Moral Dualism
and Freedom of Choice

In the beginning, *there were* two Spirits, Twins
spontaneously active,
These were the Good *and the* Evil, *in* thought, *and in* word,
and in deed.
Between these two, let the wise choose *aright*;
Be good, not base.

(Gathas: Yasna 30–3)

Moral Dualism

Asha lies at the foundation of Mazdaism; theological monotheism and moral dualism form the religion's backbones. The
doctrine of moral dualism is at one end related to the principle of
freedom of choice and at the other end to the law of consequences.

No Gathic doctrine has attracted as much attention and
aroused as much controversy as dualism. The controversy is
caused by what in psychological philosophy is called "category-
mistake," and the contending themes are "moral" and "cosmic"
dualism. The former considers Gathic dualism as a system of
thought in which good and bad are in action; and the latter relates dualism to two primordial spirits. The disputation extends
to the origin of evil and its place in the creation. Theodicy presents insoluble problems in all religions; the doctrinal adversaries

on this issue, however, admit that the Zoroastrian view of man and its solution for evil offer the most rational of all religions. "It is a complete answer that can have been reached by very clear thinking," writes Professor Hennings.[1] The development of dualism in Judaism and other Abrahamic religions is commonly attributed to the impact of the Zoroastrian religion.[2]

Dualism as used in philosophical contexts purports different things. Its most common use is in the case of body–mind relationship. The dualists believe in the existence of two different kinds of entities: body and soul (or mind). In contrast, monoists maintain that only one kind of substance, namely body, exists. Dualists also differ in their interpretation of a causal relationship between the two substances. Distinction between the visible and the invisible substance goes back to antiquity; ancestor-worship and the belief in man's higher double are evidences of that distinction.

In relationship to man, Mazdaism believes in the existence of two different worlds, *manahya* (celestial or mental) and *gaethya* (terrestrial), and two different entities, *Tanu* (body) and *Urvan* (soul or mind). Mazdaism also believes in the everlasting nature of the soul. Mazdaism maintains that mind and body (or matter, *Geteh*) are causally related.[3] Thus Zoroaster was the first to speak distinctly of the two worlds of body and soul. Plato, too, distinguished between two worlds, which he called the world of ideas and the world of matter. Unlike the world of matter, the world of ideas is not perceivable by senses. Plato knew about Zoroaster and his doctrines.[4] Before Plato, Pythagoras, who is mentioned by the Greek classical writers as a student of Zoroaster - which must have meant a student of Zoroastrianism - spoke of the transmigration of souls. Later another Greek philosopher, Anaxagoras, differentiated between matter and mind or spirit *(nous* in Greek).[5] In the seventeenth century, René Descartes introduced his theory of Cartesian dualism, and in the

---

[1] W. B. Henning, *Zoroaster*, New York: Oxford, 1951, 46.
[2] Carter, 53.
[3] The Gathas; Yasna 30-3.
[4] Willard Gurdon Oxtoby, "Interpretations of Iranian Dualism," in *Iranian Civilization and Culture,* ed. Charles J. Adams, Montreal: McGill University, 1972, 60.
[5] Ibid.

eighteenth century Georg Hegel developed his dialectical logic—the concepts of thesis, antithesis and synthesis.

The moral dualism with which we are concerned here is of a different kind. It is a mental phenomenon. It is a behavioral attitude that manifests itself in the individual's mind and conditions–the individual's actions. In this context the term *dualism* was first coined by Thomas Hyde in 1700, and later entered the metaphysical realm via Christian Wolff.[6] Thus dualism by itself may have either an ethical or metaphysical connotation.

Besides the content, the two conflicting doctrines differ on the source, nature, and significance of evil, and on the question of the management of the world's affairs. One regards dualism as a cosmic conflict, the other as ethical; one considers evil as metaphysical and independent of man, the other as a phenomenon arising from man's choice; one sees the world order as regulated by the law of *Asha* (God's will), the other as the result of the simultaneous management of Ohrmozd and Ahriman. Thus the doctrinal divergence has far-reaching consequences.

The genesis of this dual dualism may be traced to some passages in the *Gathas*. Subsequently, cosmic dualism received support from certain statements in *The Younger Avesta* (*Vendidad*) and the Pahlavi books. A paraphrased translation of the often quoted Gathic passage reads: "At the *beginning,* the twin *Mainyus* appeared together in thought, word, and deed; they were spontaneously active and in disagreement with each other; they were as the better and bad. When they came in contact, life and nonlife were established. From these two, the wise person chooses right and the unwise does the reverse." In other stanzas, the best existence is predicted for the followers of Good and the worst for the adherents of evil. In this and other Gathic passages, Zoroaster speaks of a system of thinking that dominates and directs our behavior in life. In *The Younger Avesta* and Pahlavi books, the ethical dualism converts itself into cosmic dualism-a development contrary to the Gathic tradition, according to a Zoroastrian school of thought.

The controversy over the construction of the relevant passage in the *Gathas* hinges on two key words-*beginning* and *Mainyu.* In the ongoing process of creation, does the word *beginning* refer to the inception of creation or to the appearance of human beings

---

[6] Zaehner, *The Dawn*, 45.

in the world? Does *Mainyu* mean "mentality" and "morale" or
does it connote a spirit exterior to man's mind?

The creation has no beginning; manifestation of god's creativity has. Creation always has been with God and God never has
been devoid of creativity (or constructiveness). God and *Spenta
Mainyu* (God's creativity), having no beginning, are primeval.
Destructiveness is not primeval; it has a beginning. Destruction
is non-construction and destructive power is activated by human
agency when man fails his constructive power. Thus beginning
refers to the birth of man. And *Mainyu* signifies man's mentality.
Even if *Mainyus* are exterior to man, they cannot be primordial.
The *Mainyu* that creates life, and all good things, emanates from
Ahura Mazda; nonlife (which we may call de-creation), and all
bad things in the world, manifest themselves when a creation of
Ahura Mazda fails to act in harmony with the law of creation.
Consequently, Zoroastrian monotheism is not a qualified one.
The interrelationship of the two spirits is essential to a true un-
derstanding of their nature and function in the Zoroastrian per-
spective of creation.

For the following reasons the word *beginning* cannot refer to
creation.

First, admitting the immutability of God and his attributes, we
must concede that by definition, God cannot be devoid of his
creativity. *Spenta Mainyu*, God's creativity, is the most distinguishing feature of *Ahura Mazda* and is closely related to him.
Sometimes the two are considered identical. The constant association of *Ahura Mazda* and *Spenta Mainyu* has led some western scholars to compare the relationship between *Spenta Mainyu*
and *Ahura Mazda* in the *Gathas* to that of the Holy Ghost and
the Father in the New Testament.[7] In his Good Mind, through
Spenta Mainyu (the Good and Holy Spirit), *Ahura Mazda* creates.

Secondly, considering that the creation was not made *ex nihil*
and that man was not the first creature of God, we realize that the
word *beginning* must refer to the birth of man. The words used
in the *Gathas* for creation are *giving* and *shaping* (or *designing*).
Creation is as old as God himself; the shape and design of the
creatures evolve, change, and progress according to the law of
Asha. Man appeared in the course of the evolution of creation as

---

[7] Dhalla, *History*, 34, 39, 40.

it was willed by God. The Semitic story of Adam and Eve does not exist in the *Gathas*; though the myth of the Creation of the first man and woman (in a different form) appears in the later religious literature.

Thirdly, God is the Being without a beginning, which requires the absence of non-Being. Therefore, the word *beginning* in the above cited stanza cannot relate to God. By the same token, the twin *Mainyu* cannot be primordial. In the *Gathas*, nothing is primordial but *Ahura Mazda*, his attributes and *Spenta Mainyu*. This fact is evident from many passages. Furthermore, Zoroaster repeatedly affirms that *Ahura Mazda* is the only Being who existed from the beginning. This is a positive statement; it repudiates any suggestion that "as evidence, the argument for Zoroaster as a monotheist is an argument from silence."[8] In stating a reality one does not have to deny all the unreals!

What does *mainyu* mean in the relevant Gathic stanza? *Mainyu* derives from *Mana*, meaning mentality and wisdom. It also means spirit. If spirit and mind are interchangeable, no difficulty arises; the passages would simply mean that at the beginning of the appearance of man, the two spirits or mentalities simultaneously manifested themselves in man's mind. One was Good and the other evil. Man has the freedom to choose between the two, follow one and ignore the other. Freedom presupposes alternatives. The two spirits represent the two diametrically opposed courses of action. As stated at the outset, the principle of moral dualism at one end is closely linked to the principle of freedom of choice and at the other end to the principle of consequences, commonly known as the principle of reward and punishment. The latter principle is a corollary of the law of *Asha*. A man who opts for good will embraces success and happiness—one who prefers evil will suffer failure and misery. In the *Gathas*, the principle of moral dualism is mentioned either in association with man's spontaneousness and freedom of action or in relation to sequences and effects. In the *Gathas*, evil has no manifestation exterior to man's thought, word, and deed. It is stated in the *Gathas* that no reconciliation between good and evil and no accommodation of wicked thought, word, deed, beliefs, and teachings by the righteous is possible. Zoroaster alerts his audience to the fact that the best in life is to act in consonance

---

[8] Oxtoby, 64.

ence to the fact that the best in life is to act in consonance with the spirit of truth.[9]

To the extent that the principle is explained here, no ambiguity exists. Evil is the opposite of good or, in the words of the *Gathas*, it is the non-good. No goodness in creation is perceivable without its opposite. In this sense, good and evil in this world become matters of function and not substance. They do not have any substance outside the realm of man's thought, word, and deed. In the transcendence, the Sublime Good prevails and good in this world is only a reflection of the Absolute Goodness. In Mazdaism, matter is not the outward manifestation of an idea, form, or spirit; and evil is not related to any transcendent reality. Mind and matter are both real.

Two other factors have contributed to the confusion over Zoroastrian dualism. One is the fact that *Ahura Mazda* in his creativity works through *Spenta Mainyu*, his holy and good spirit; the other is the strong moral character of *Ahura Mazda* and consequently of *Spenta Mainyu*. The moral content of God is so representative that *Ahura Mazda* appears only in his moral attributes, and not in flesh (as in Christianity) or in fire (as in Judaism). The *Gathas* do not give a proper name to the evil spirit. It gives the epithet of *angra* to such spirits. Thus, the *Gathas* place *Angra Mainyu*, the evil spirits in this world in opposition to *Spenta Mainyu*, the good spirit in his worldly function, and not directly against *Ahura Mazda* in his celestial position. Recalling that *Spenta Mainyu* poses as God's Spirit, the ensuing confusion, placing Ahriman in direct opposition as counterpart to Ohrmozd, is not surprising.

Symbolically light represents God and darkness evil, but it is erroneous to think of darkness as a creation of evil–as it has been asserted by certain scholars. The *Gathas* do not give the name of any creator other than *Ahura Mazda* for the worldly elements and atmospheric phenomena. In the *Gathas*, *Ahura Mazda* is named as the creator of both light and darkness.[10] I shall further explain this point in connection with evil.

---

[9] The *Gathas*; *Yasnas* 45-2, 3, 4, 5; 30-5, 6.
[10] The *Gathas*; Yasna 44-5.

Evil

The nature of evil in Zoroastrianism has generated heated arguments among the students of the religion. The ambiguity in the construction of the relevant passages in the *Gathas* has already been discussed. Here we address ourselves to some passages in the three Pahlavi books of Dinkard, Bundahishn, and *Shikand Gumani Vijar*. The views on evil explained in these books represent a complete change from ethical to cosmic dualism. Such deviations are not unusual in other religious traditions. We must bear in mind that these books were written over two centuries after the Arab invasion and contain some important philosophical theories of the Sassanian time. At the time of the composition of these books Manichaean and other heretic thinking still had a hold on the intellectual elite. The confused presentation of the arguments in segments of the books is indicative of the pressure under which the authors have composed their works. From the arguments set out in those books two major schools may be recognized.

1. The first school maintains that evil is a function of a depraved mind. It has no substance independent of man's mind and action. Creation is an ongoing process and *Spenta Mainyu* represents its dynamism. Creation in reference to its dynamism evolves. New creations appear and the old ones are replaced and transformed. Some old creations cease to have corporeal existence. The human being was not one of the first creations. In the Zoroastrian story of genesis composed by Pahlavi writers, humans were created one year after the creation of the universe. How many years that mythical one year represents is hard to say. According to *The Younger Avestan* tradition, man, *Mashya*, and woman, *Mashyoi*, appeared from the evolution and transformation of a "twin plant" originally grown in the ground from the seed of the Gayo Marata, the prototype of man.[11]

The term *Angra Mainyu*, which is translated as "evil spirit", means evil mentality. It is this mentality that, together with its opposite twin, *Spenta Mainyu*, in his worldly function, manifests itself spontaneously in human beings; each person has to make

---

[11] John R. Hinnels, *Persian Mythology* (London: The Hamlyn Publishing House, 1973), 59, 60.

his or her choice between the two. In the realm of transcendence and the absolute, *Spenta Mainyu* has no opposite. It is in the world of relativity, in the creation of free man, that its opposite manifests itself through man's free choice. With erroneous choice human beings create and activate evil in themselves and in society. It is not evil as an extraneous entity, but as an internal element, that overtakes man. If all human beings made right choices and led righteous lives there would be no evil. *Angra Mainyu* is used as a generic, and not a proper, noun in the *Avesta.*[12]

The adherents of this school, whom we call monotheists, further argue that in the *Gathas*, *Ahura Mazda* is the first and the last (or more accurately without a beginning and an end), the primordial, the all-wise and the all-powerful. Recognition of a counterpart opposite for *Ahura* Mazda amounts to the negation of one of the most fundamental Gathic doctrines. Evil as a substance extraneous to man, they maintain, does not exist. God knew that some people would opt for wickedness; this is a price man has to pay for the enjoyment of the liberty. In the order of creation, freedom of thought and action is so precious that it should not be abandoned for the fear of wicked inclinations by a few persons. The final triumph of good over evil, which is a feature of God's omnipotence, removes the anxieties that may result from the acts of the few wicked.[13] Finally, monotheists forcefully argue that had the twin spirits not appeared and not been confronted in man's mind, nonlife would not have come into being.[14] The inference also is that prior to that confrontation in man's mind, the opposite counterpart of *Spenta Mainyu* did not exist. It is man who in his finitude experiences the opposite of existence as death. Therefore evil relates to man's experiences. The absence of the evil spirit before creation of the world, indicates that it is not primordial.

2. The second school, which conveniently may be called dualistic, argues that evil is a substantive entity and not a functional incident. The adherents of this school consider the evil to be primeval and as a result, there are two creators: one creating good and the other producing evil. They however maintain that

---

[12] Dhalla, *History*, 89.

[13] The *Gathas*; *Yasnas* 48-2; 47-6.

[14] The Gathas; Yasna 30-4.

evil, not being omniscient, did not know that a good God existed; the good God knew of the presence of evil. Evil, only after seeing the good God's creations, became aware of good God's existence. Then evil tried to make counterparts of what good God had made. For light, evil produced darkness; for cleanliness defilement; for truth falsehood; and the like. According to the *Gathas*, however, it was God who created both lightness and darkness, day and night, and the cosmic order. None of God's creations is evil; man can use them for good and evil purposes. Symbolically darkness represents evil, but this should not imply that darkness is evil. The dualists maintain that evil could not make the counterpart of a human being since God had produced man in his attributive image. God deposited in man a gleam of his attributes–goodness. Evil is incapable of making anything good. So evil made every attempt to deceive man and turn him against God. The dualists concede, however, that at the end, good will prevail and this event will constitute the establishment of God's kingdom (an ideal society) on earth.

The dualists emphatically claim the concept discussed above represents the orthodox Zoroastrian doctrine and that it is the only rational explanation of evil that does not bring into doubt the goodness and justice of God. They claim that in the early stages of history good God was not omnipotent, but at the end he will attain that position. They further argue that evil cannot be only a passive negation of good; it is an active force. In their zeal to personify evil, the dualists have classified the noxious insects and poisonous plants as productions of evil and, as such, they become evil. In Pahlavi books, the noxious creations of evil are called *Khrafstra*, creeping things. The dualists claim that the existence of wild beasts and harmful animals can only be ascribed to evil; they cannot be explained away by the mentality theory.

In the Pahlavi books, the good God is designated as Ohrmozd and the evil one as Ahriman. Ohrmozd is the source of light, truth, goodness, and joy; Ahriman is the producer of darkness, lies, and misery. Ohrmozd is constructive and Ahriman destructive. The corollary is that the two sources are primordial, antipodal, and function independently. Man as Ohrmozd's coworker must emulate him and struggle against Ahriman.

On the authority of the Pahlavi philosophical writings, the dualists assert that Ohrmozd cannot be infinite in all respects, since Ahriman is also a primal source. They conclude that

"Ohrmozd is infinite with time and limited with space ... Originally, then, he is eternal but not infinite ... Ahriman is bounded by both space and time ... (Ohrmozd is only bound by space because he must share the space with Ahriman and the void [space] which lies between the two kingdoms.) "[15] In the same Pahlavi book, Bundahishn, it is stated that, "It is revealed in the Good Religion that Ohrmozd was on high in omniscience and goodness: for infinite time he was ever in the light. The light is the space and the place of Ohrmozd: some call it the Endless Light. Omniscience and goodness are the permanent disposition of Ohrmozd: some call them 'Religion.' The interpretation of both is the same, namely the permanent disposition of the infinite Time, for Ohrmozd and Space, Religion, and Time of Ohrmozd were and are and evermore shall be."[16] Bundahishn is undoubtedly a sensationally intellectual and philosophical treatise, yet it is not free of contradictions. In one place it says "Ohrmozd in his omniscience knew that the Destructive Spirit existed,"[17] and in another place it states that the omniscience of Ohrmozd, too, is finite. "Concerning the finite and infinite:" Bundahishn says, "the heights which are called the Endless Light (since they have no end) and the depths which are Endless Darkness, these are infinite. On the border, both are finite since between them is the Void, and there is no contact between the two." This quotation, of course, relates to space, but it continues: "Again both Spirits in themselves are finite. Again concerning the omniscience of Ohrmozd–everything that is within the knowledge of Ohrmozd is finite."[18] The contradiction in these passages weakens its authority. Bundahishn states that evil takes abode for eternity in the abyss of endless darkness.

Mardan Farruk, the author of the ninth-century Pahlavi work, *Shikand Gumani Vijar*, also denies the omnipotence of Ohrmozd. "Ohrmozd is like the owner or a gardener in whose garden noxious and destructive beasts and birds are intent on doing harm to its fruits and trees. And the wise gardener, to save himself trouble and to keep those noxious beasts out of the garden, devises means to capture them."[19] He also refutes Manichaeanism for

---

[15] Zaehner, *The Dawn,* 29, 30.

[16] *Bundahishn*, ch. 1, para. 1.

[17] Ibid., para. 5.

[18] Ibid., para. 14.

[19] Shikand Gumani Vijar, ch. 5, para. 63.

equating evil with matter, for believing in the satanic nature of the world, and for advocating asceticism, all of which he considers anti-Zoroastrian. Likewise, he criticizes Islam and Christianity for ascribing the creation of evil to God and, by so doing, undermining the goodness of their Gods. He rejects the concept of evil as a state of privation (a concept claimed by Christians). Finally, he considers "evil a reality, a pure spirit and the negation of life."[20] On the other hand, he says "evil is wrong-mindedness, stupidity, blind self-assertiveness, error," by which he means following evil is the essence of wrong-mindedness. Mardan Farruk also divides the contraries into two groups: those whose difference is in principle like light and darkness, and those whose difference is in function or nature like male and female. The distinction is that contraries in principle or substance cannot mix. They are antagonistic to each other: where light appears, darkness disappears. But contraries in function can coexist and collaborate. The author further states, "the wise, omniscient, and omnipotent Creator is self-sufficing, and his perfection consists in his having no needs for any advantage or increase which he might desire from outside. So we must conclude that the reason and the occasion for his actions must all be of one kind–to repel and ward off whatever damage might accrue to him from an external adversary who could harm him; and this is the whole reason and occasion for the act of creation."[21] Thus he does not believe in the omnipotence of God during his confrontation with Ahriman, although he recognizes God's perfection, which in his view is God's freedom from need. He says God needs to create in order to defend himself.

Another line of reasoning taken by dualists is that "as in the material world contrary substances exist and ... they are sometimes mutually cooperative and sometimes mutually destructive, so [they must exist] in the spiritual world, which is the cause of material, and material things are their effect ... The material world is the effect of the spiritual and the spiritual is its cause."[22] The mutually cooperative contraries may refer to mixed cases.

The difference between the two schools, as described, is colossal. One believes that evil is mentality and is dependent on

---

[20] Ibid., ch. 8, paras 2, 7, 23, 89, 124.

[21] Ibid., paras 49-51.

[22] Ibid., paras 35-37.

man and activated by man; the other maintains that it is spirit and primordial. One asserts that evil is the negative of good and is activated when man refuses to do good or does the opposite of good; the other holds that evil has a separate entity and is extraneous to man. One affirms unity in the cosmos and eternity; the other disunity and duality in both. One considers evil as a functional incident; the other as a substantive matter. One considers spirit and matter realities in their own spheres; the other regards spirit as the cause of matter. One believes in the absoluteness and harmony of the spiritual, and the relativity and disharmony of the physical world; the other in the mutually cooperative and destructive nature of both spiritual and material worlds. In contrast to the said differences, both schools agree on two things: man is a coworker with God and the ultimate triumph belongs to goodness.

The doctrinal controversy over evil is ancient. The writer of the Pahlavi book of *Shikand Gumani Vijar* criticizes those who maintain that evil springs from the nature of man. His reasoning in the rejection of this theory is flawed. He says acceptance of the theory that man through freedom of choice created evil, amounts to defiance of the will of his creator and, therefore, is not possible.[23] Indeed the *Gathas* repeatedly state that evildoers are defying God and acting against the law, which is the same as his will. The writer of *Shikand Gumani* argues that God would not create his adversary; but he fails to see that being of man's making, evil would not be a creature of God. The arguments that he uses for the omniscience, omnipotence, and justice of God are self-defeating. He argues that with an independent existence of evil as a primordial spirit, God can remain all-powerful!

The theory that evil is the result of man's erroneous choice and that it springs from man's mentality removes all the objections to an all-perfect God and preserves God's grandeur. Man's freedom of choice, inherent in the law of *Asha*, is God's Will. Being a good God, he has given freedom of choice to man. He has not created evil. The end victory of goodness indicates God's omnipotence. God is just and wants all human beings to be just and righteous. He has sent his prophet to guide man. The argument that God has created evil so that mankind may better understand and appreciate goodness is not a Zoroastrian doctrine.

---

[23] Ibid., paras 117, 124-134.

Nor is the statement in the *Dinkard* that Ohrmozd has allowed evil to comingle with his creation for an allotted period for the experience and training of mankind.[24] God has no need to put man to the test.

Shikand Gumani's author, an ardent dualist philosopher-theologian, concludes that dualism exists not only in the physical world, but also in the spiritual realm; that in all parts evil is stronger than good. He further states that things in the world are either good, bad, or a mixture of both. This conclusion amounts to the introduction of relativity into the spiritual world, because according to him this world, in structure, resembles the other. Again, in Mazdaism, as we have indicated before, matter and mind have their own existence and both are real. The body is not an outward feature of the soul, nor are they two sides of the same coin.

It is wrong to dismiss either of the two schools as irrelevant. The two questions here are: (i) what school represents Zoroastrian orthodoxy? and (ii) what is the theological and socio-political explanation for change, if any, from one theory of dualism to the other?

For the answer to the first question we must return to the *Gathas*. In that book, *Angra Mainyu* is used in a generic sense, meaning evil mentality or evil spirit. It appears with *Spenta Mainyu* as its opposite twin. *Angra* is used also as a designation for wicked person. Another term used for evil spirit is *Aka Mana*, meaning "evil mind."

Daevas, the gods of Indo-Iranians, and their worshippers are called *Aka Mana*.[25] *Druj*, meaning falsehood, is used for violators of the law of *Asha*. These terminologies do not imply the external or primordial qualities of evil. They only indicate that in this world evil is real. On the balance of evidence, it seems that the monotheistic school is more congruous with the spirit of the *Gathas* and that *Angra Mainyu* originates in man's mind and in this world through man's erroneous choice.

In *The Younger Avesta* the situation changes and the personality of evil becomes more pronounced. *Angra Mainyu* assumes the role of the producer of all-destructive, harmful, and evil things, including disease, drought, famine, and plague. How did

---

[24] Denkart, ed. Madon, pp. 201-202.
[25] Dhalla, *History*, 91.

the transformation come about? What religious and socio-political factors caused the conversion to cosmic dualism? This transformation, we submit, must have been brought about by both theologians (Magi) and politically oppressed groups, either during Sassanians, in the post-Arab invasion, or both.

Theologians tried to keep *Ahura Mazda* clear of evil things in accord with the *Gathas*. The Magi, who had not lost their love for the Indo-Iranian pantheon of gods and had already incorporated *Yazatas* into *Avesta*, successfully included in the *Avesta* the pre-Zoroastrian concepts of evil in the form of *daevas* to become foes of the *Yazatas*. This innovation had emotional appeal to people and socio-economic advantage for them. Thus every *Yazata* found his or her opposite counterpart. They also made harmful animals and insects creations of demons. Herodotus and Plutarch relate that the killing of noxious creatures was recommended by the Magi.[26] This idea was reintroduced in *Vendidad*,[27] into which book myth and folklore also found their way. The treacherous king *Azhi Dahaka* was labeled an apostle of evil.[28] *Angra Mainyu* became the Demon of Demons[29] as *Ahura Mazda* was the Spirit of Spirits. Special tasks were assigned to each demon by Ahriman, the new substitute for *Angra Mainyu*. The demons spread uncleanliness, disease, famine, drought, and death. One of the means of fending off demons was to perform constructive works such as engaging in agriculture, raising cattle, and serving one's fellowmen. Such good acts were purported to dismay and defeat devils. The other means was reciting holy spells with special rites performed by the clergy. It was this last function that economically interested the clergy. The performance of such religious ceremonies also gave the Magis a greater social influence. About such rites Plutarch writes that demons (*daevas*) were elemental powers which could be more or less successfully manipulated by the appropriate rites and magic formulas.[30] The antithesis between good and bad soon found its way into the vocabulary used by the Magi. The good spoke, ate, and walked, while the evil howled, devoured, and rushed; the good had a head and lived in a house, while the evil had a skull and

---

[26] Herodotus 1, 30.

[27] *Vendidad*, 19, 1-3.

[28] *Vendidad*, 4, 47.

[29] *Vendidad*, 19, 1, 43.

[30] Dhalla, 258.

dwelled in a burrow.[31] The Pahlavi writers enlarged the domains of authority of the two opposite powers.

During the Sassanians, the controversy between the two schools must have mounted. Manichaeanism and Mazdakism, both condemning wealth, power, and luxury, appealed to the poor and the oppressed; both religions propagated cosmic dualism. Zurvanism lent philosophical support to cosmic dualism. Whatever the reasons for change, during the Sassanians, Ahriman was established as the greatest villain spirit with an independent personality. It became the source of all evils in the world. Thus evil became invisible and primordial. Ahriman's nature could be understood, but he could not be seen, However, Arda Viraf in his apocalyptic journey to hell–Ahriman's abode– saw him in person. It is interesting that for the first time Ahriman in that book appears as both a snake and a lizard, which clearly shows the influence of other religions on the Mazdaism of the Sassanian period. In addition to death, disease, misery, poison, and biting creatures, Ahriman produced falsehood and six chief demons, the direct adversaries of *Amesha Spentas*. They were *Aka Mana* (evil mind), *Indar* (perversion and falsehood), *Sovar* (tyranny and violence), *Nakahed* (disobedience and enmity), *Taire* (imperfection), and *Zairich* (destruction and death).[32] "It is suffering and death (or the demons) that destroy the body, not the creator whose will is good and who preserves and maintains the body," writes Mardan Farruk.[33]

The dualist theory can be supported neither by the *Gathas* nor by the beliefs of the most practicing Zoroastrians. No Zoroastrian would ascribe the creation of Khrafstra to Ahriman. Ahriman is the object of constant condemnation, not as a creator, but as a phenomenon. In the finite and relative world no concept without its opposite is perceivable by man. This does not make the opposite primordial. To draw a parallel, in the Old Testament it is stated that when God created light, he separated it from darkness. This statement does not make darkness, or satan, primordial.

To a practicing Zoroastrian the conception of Ahriman or evil corresponds to that in the Iranian epic tradition. Asked about the

[31] Ibid. 309-403.
[32] Ibid. 399-406.
[33] *Shikand Gumani Vijar,* ch. 8, paras 57, 71, 78, 103, 104, 120-123, 132-134.

nature of evil, a Zoroastrian uses the terms *Div* and *Druj*. Div is used in a generic sense, depicting a huge monster. Druj means falsehood. Div and Druj are neither spirits nor depraved angels. To Zoroastrians all wicked and undesirable acts, thoughts, and words cluster around the concept of Div and Druj.

In *Shahnameh*, the great epic history of pre-Islamic Iran, Div is portrayed as an obnoxiously powerful creature.[34] Lying is its symbolic characteristic. He talks and acts in an evil manner. For the sake of destruction, he wants to harm everybody and everything. Complete lack of intelligence is another characteristic of Div. He cannot discern the consequences of his actions. He does the reverse of whatever is suggested to him. In the *Shahnameh*, the great hero, Rustam, encounters Div Akvan and Div Spid. Akvan is the same as Aka Mana, meaning evil mind. Spid means white and perhaps Div-e-Sepid alludes to the evil people who act like wolves in sheep's clothing. In Zoroastrianism, symbolically, the color white is associated with goodness and the color black with wickedness.

Div wants to kill Rustam and asks him which of the two alternative forms of death he would prefer: to be thrown over the mountains and be eaten by beasts, or be thrown in the sea and be drowned and swallowed by whales. Div's intention is to make Rustam die the worst possible death. Rustam, who was intelligent and a skilled swimmer, proposed to be thrown into the mountains. Div thrust Rustam into the sea and Rustam managed to reach the shore safely. A thousand years ago, Ferdowsi, the author of the *Shahnameh*, wrote that Div and Ahriman were not but wicked persons.[35] In other words, he says that they are not metaphysical or spiritual creatures. This story presents the image of Div or Satan as it is perceived by a devout lay Zoroastrian today. Div is not transcendent; he lies and is ill-willed. The story of Adam, Eve, Satan and the fallen man, as stated in Abrahamic religions, does not exist in Mazdaism, and therefore comparison in form and substance of Ahriman with Satan would be misleading.

Whatever the true interpretation of the Gathic doctrine of dualism, Zoroaster is the founder of the philosophy of mind, a topic

---

[34] Shahneme Ferdawssi.
[35] See footnote 29, chapter 3.

that has absorbed many great thinkers including Plato, Aristotle, René Descartes, George Hegel and others.

Freedom of Choice

The precepts of Mazdaism are grounded in Truth and Justice (*Asha*), connected with Wisdom (*Vohu Mana*), and imbued with liberalism and free choice. Zoroaster preached to his audience to accept the faith freely, to elect their path wisely, and to choose their friends, teachers and life consorts intelligently. Seldom has a revealed religion exhibited such liberality.

Zoroaster recognized the individuality and uniqueness of each individual, and at the same time emphasized man's collective identity through membership in his family, community, country, and religion. Although unique, man and his destiny are interwoven with the life and destiny of the universe, the earth, and the environment, and as such man must preserve and promote life on earth. These points of identity are inserted in Zoroastrian daily prayers.[36] In the realm of faith, Zoroaster said that acceptance of faith should be associated with conviction. Profession of faith without conviction is futile. To free his followers from the yoke of self-interested clergy, he opposed obsessive rituals, stood for simplicity in prayers, and stated that everybody through righteousness can establish communication with God. For man, he resolved the problem of life and death, happiness and misery. Unlike most of the world's religions, Mazdaism gave women equal status with men. It rose against illiteracy and ignorance and condemned intimidation and oppression. The acceptance of a religion should be according to one's own conscience.

According to the *Gathas*, *Ahura Mazda* in his conscience, *Daena*, created life and granted man the faculties to choose between good and bad, and the power to think, talk, and act.[37] *Daena* also connotes religion, and the aforementioned declaration means that God in his religious practice fashioned man. He gave man *Vohu Mana*, good (holy) mind. This is the faculty with which man can think and reason before making a decision. He

---

[36] Waterhouse, 81.
[37] Ibid., 82.

also gave man conscience, *Daena*. This is the moral faculty with which man can pursue a righteous and ethical life. *The Younger Avesta* talks about another faculty bestowed upon man, enlightenment or *Baodha*. With these three faculties man should be able to distinguish right from wrong and virtuousness from wickedness. There are sensory as well as extrasensory faculties. *Daena* is man's self.[38] It is the internalized image of the self that includes an ability to evaluate societal, normative belief systems.

Implied in the *Avesta* is a good deal of psychology. In Mazdaism man's personality is formed by six elements: Ego (*Daena*), Mind (*Mana*), Perception (*Baodha*), Being = Vitality (*Ahu*), the guardian spirit (*Fravashi*), and divine grace (*Xvarengha*).[39] *Daena* is conscience or the individual's sense of responsibility. It is the individual's ego that determines his destiny. *Fravashi* is not mentioned in the *Gathas*. *Daena* is affected by the thoughts, words, and deeds of man. When man dies, according to *Yashts*, his *Daena* awaits him at the dividing line of the two worlds–the Bridge of Judgment (*Chinvat*).[40] In the case of a virtuous person, it appears in the form of a beautiful maiden, and in the case of a wicked person in the shape of an ugly fiend.[41] Each individual is directed by his or her *Daena* to heaven (the best abode) or to hell (the worst abode). The *Gathas* state that each person by his or her own inclinations and by his or her free choice determines the mode of his or her life. An individual freely shapes his or her thoughts, words, and deeds. Consequently, one's *Daena*, through one's free choice, turns good or evil. So *Daena* represents the inner self. In the words of the *Gathas*, the best *Daena* is the best religion.[42]

Mind, *Mana*, has already been defined. It is the source of holy or good wisdom. Good is synonymous with holy. *Baodha* is the means of perception. It represents enlightenment. Enlightenment comes through meditation and personal mystical experience. It is intuitive. The *Dinkard* says, "As the sun illumines the world, Baodha enlightens the man. It is a watchful light that animates the lord of the house to take care of the house."[43] *Ahu*,

[38] Ibid., 83.
[39] Dhalla, *History*, 232-235.
[40] The Gathas; Yasna 46-10.
[41] *Yasht* 22-9, 25.
[42] *Dinkard* vi, 354.
[43] Waterhouse, 79.

being, life, and vitality, has been "paralleled by the modern conception of Life-Urge or Elan Vital."[44] *Ahu* is applicable to both the soul and the body, but in this context it coexists with the body and its function is to hold the soul and the body together. The body transforms when *Ahu* no longer dwells in it. *Fravashi* is a more complex concept. For the reason stated below, the *Gathas* do not mention it. But in the *Avesta*, the *Fravashi* of righteous men together with their *Ahu*, *Baodha* and *Daena*, are adored.[45] The *Fravashis* of virtuous people are adored because they have been victorious in winning the path of truth for their possessors. *Fravashi* literally means confession. *Fravashi* remains good and, unlike *Daena*, is not adversely affected by the deeds of its possessor. No reference to the *Fravashis* of the wicked is ever made in the *Avesta*. My conclusion is that the *Fravashi* of the lost soul leaves the body. *Fravashis* perhaps "are the prototypes of all life, both of man and of beast, existing before creation."[46] *Fravashi* may be considered a gleam of God in every creature, be it human beings or animals. *Fravashi* is goodness. *Daena* dwells only in human beings. *Fravashis* are also said to be the guardian spirits of birth.

The absence of *Fravashi* in the *Gathas* is not accidental. *Fravashi* is believed to be a remnant of the cult of ancestor-worship predominant in many primitive societies including pre-Mazdaism Iran. Zoroaster must have deliberately excluded it from the *Gathas* to keep monotheism intact. It was revived by the Magi as a spirit-guardian. Dastur Dr Dhalla likens *Fravashi* to Plato's concept of "idea," the Roman idea of *Genii*, the Egyptian notion of *Ka*, and the Brahmanic element of *Atman*. Dhalla himself must have been conscious of the limitation of such comparisons because he immediately states that in Brahmanism every creature, good or bad, has *Atman*, but in *Avesta* only the good have *Fravashi*. All this is mentioned here to remove the erroneous concept of some Western scholars that *Fravashi* represents *Ahura Mazda*. Such a view is totally untenable.[47]

The festival in honor of *Fravashis* of the departed souls, observed by Zartushtis of Iran and the Parsees of India and Paki-

---

[44] *Yasht* 13-155.
[45] Dhalla, *History*, 235.
[46] Ibid., 333.
[47] Waterhouse, 82.

stan, is likened to the Christian All Souls' Day.[48] It is also associated with many rituals that recall the requirement of precise performance, such as those in the Indian *Pitaras* and the Roman *Manes*.[49] The possible influence of the concept of *Frarashi* in both Talmud and New Testament has been alluded to by certain scholars,[50] showing its universality in one form or another.

With the faculties bestowed upon them, human beings should be able to discern good from evil and to choose the right path. The body, being a physical object, cannot act without the soul and the faculties vouchsafed to it. While in Mazdaism matter and spirit are two separate substances, they interact. The mind affects the body. In the mutual interaction, the preponderance is with the mind, though the body, too, can condition the mind. Each has its own qualities, and both are creations of God. Man has a special place in relationship to matter and mind. He has the choice to employ them for his happiness and the progress of the world, or for the destruction of both. The world is God's creation, and it is governed by the same law that governs the activities of mind. This pronounced dualism, misunderstood by many, has caused them to think of Mazdaism as a dualist religion. Theologically it is monotheistic; morally it is dualistic. It takes evil out of the realm of the infinite and absolute and allocates it to the realm of finite man. Man can and ought to hinder the appearance of evil. In the *Gathas* Zoroaster, addressing God, says: "O, Mazda! From the beginning, through your own Wisdom, you fashioned *Daena*, conscience, for man with which to discern and *Mana*, wisdom, with which to direct his acts; and you granted him power to think, talk, and act so that he can choose his beliefs."[51] This is the principle of the freedom of choice enunciated in the *Gathas*.

Positive and negative, thesis and antithesis, mind and matter, and every other sense in which dualism has been used, Zoroastrian dualism only relates to the mind and to freedom of choice. It connotes the two antipodal attitudes, postures, prototypes, natures, dispositions, characters, spirits, moralities, and mentalities in the spiritual framework. They are neither complementary nor can they produce a synthesis. They are irreconcilable and cannot

---

[48] Dhalla, 236; Zaehner, *The Dawn,* 78, 81; J. H. Moulton, Early *Zoroastrianism,* quoted by Waterhouse, 84, 85.
[49] Dhalla, *History,* 237.
[50] Ibid. 242.
[51] The Gathas; Yasna 31-11.

associate with each other. They disagree in comprehension, beliefs, words, and deeds. They oppose each other at every step.
For this reason man must make his choice intelligently, definitely, and unambiguously. This distinction is vitally important
for a true understanding of Zoroastrian freedom of choice in relationship to dualism.

Manichaeanism is also uncompromisingly dualistic, but it
equates evil with matter and good with spirit. This is an aberration of Zoroastrian dualism. "Manichaeanism profoundly affected Islamic mysticism, and through St. Augustine has left
traces in Christianity,"[52] and seemingly in some of the Zoroastrian writers of the Sassanian period. There is a distinct difference between Mazdaism, which sees the whole creation as good,
and religions that consider this world satanic. Any corruption in
the world is subsequent to the appearance of man in the universe;
it is the result of man's erroneous choice. That mistaken choice is
equivalent to evil.

The wickedness of man is the reality of Ahriman in
Mazdaism.[53] This fact is the solution to the enigma of why a
good and omniscient God should create evil! The answer is that
man and not God creates evil. God either had to make man a
slave without freedom of choice, or grant him freedom and let
the wicked suffer as the result of his mistaken option. Zoroastrian sages have always maintained that God, the Perfect Being,
cannot originate an imperfect creation.[54] Therefore imperfection
of evil is the work of imperfect man.

To conclude, moral dualism is the reality of life. God created
the mental and the physical worlds. Everything created by God is
good. God's creations in their manifestation in the mental and
physical worlds appear as opposite twins; God himself has no
twin. If it is used to imply two creators, cosmic dualism does not
exist in Zoroastrianism; mental dualism does. If used to purport
the opposite or complementary phenomenon in this world, cosmic dualism does exist. Hence *Spenta Mainyu* manifests itself
with *Angra Mainyu*–good with evil. Angra Mainyu represents

---

[52] "Manichaeism . . . attracted the interest of theologians and more than
one mystic was accused of Manachaen inclinations." Anne Marie
Schimmel, *Mystical Dimensions of Islam* (Chapel Hill: The University
of North Carolina Press, 1975), 34.
[53] Shikand Gumani Vijar, ch. viii, 103-106.
[54] Ibid., 107.

deviation from Spenta Mainyu. The *Gathas* preach the worship of one God, *Ahura Mazda,* and the ceaseless struggle against evil. The *Gathas* refer to the evil that appears in man's thought, word, and deed. Man as coworker of *Ahura Mazda* must refrain from wickedness and relentlessly oppose it. The manifestation of *Ahura Mazda* in his cardinal moral attributes means the appearance of the *Spenta Mainyu*-the Holy Creative Spirit of *Ahura Mazda* with all the cardinal qualities–as God's image in this world. The creation of man in God's attributive image as his co-worker; and the uniquely ethical nature of Mazdaism made the transformation of moral dualism into cosmic dualism (in the sense of the existence of two creators, in *The Younger Avesta* and Pahlavi literature) possible. Moral dualism, the existence of good and evil, is a fact of life that a Zoroastrian must face and overcome.

V

THE CREATIVE (HOLY) SPIRIT: *SPENTA MAINYU*

The Principle of Bounteous Creation

This Holy Spirit's Father *true art Thou,*
Thou didst create this earth to give us joy;
And Thou didst send Armaity to protect,
She brings us peace, whenever filled with Love,
Witb Vohu Mana, *Mazda we commune.*

(Gathas: Yasna 47–3)

Spenta Mainyu

Spenta Mainyu is an attribute, yet the quintessence, of God. It's the holy, good, bounteous, and creative Spirit of God. It is God and yet distinct from God. It acts as coworker and vicere-gent of God. It is the manifestation of God's creative will and thought.[1] It is the reality of God's goodness and holiness. It is God's son, yet it has always been with the Father. It is as old as *Ahura Mazda* himself, since time has no relevance to it; *Spenta Mainyu* has no beginning and no end.

Spenta means augmentative, bounteous, good, and creative. It is also translated as "holy." *Spenta Mainyu* is Holy Spirit in that it is godly and in the service of God and deserves man's absolute adoration. It is perfect, immortal, transcendent, and immanent. It

---

[1] Dhalla, *History*, 36.

unfolds the immanence of God in its fullness; it represents the bounteousness of god in its plentitude. It unveils God's abundance. "Holiness for Zoroaster also meant abundance, growth, and health."[2] Zoroastrianism blesses all the good things of this world as well as the other world.

Mainyu means spirit and/or mentality. Mind and spirit, if not identical, are inseparably interwoven. Mentality is the functional aspect of the spirit. *Spenta Mainyu* in its immanence manifests itself in man's good thought, good word, and good deed. An individual who in his mind opts to oppose *Spenta Mainyu* becomes evil or *Angra Mainyu*. *Angra Mainyu* is *Spenta Mainyu's* opponent and God's adversary. An individual who turns evil is no longer a coworker of God, as he has violated God's law. *Angra Mainyu* is not created by God nor is it transcendent. It is the mentality or the spirit of disobedience and represents conscious revolt against the law of *Asha*. *Spenta Mainyu* is the drive to promote Righteous order, *Angra Mainyu* is the drive to frustrate it.

Spenta Mainyu and *Ahura Mazda*

Ahura Mazda and *Spenta Mainyu*, though of the same will, are not identical. Though the six cardinal attributes of God include holiness and bounteousness, God's parenthood relationship to *Spenta Mainyu* is more emphasized than his parenthood to the six other cardinal attributes–good mind, truth, divine sovereignty, love, perfection, and immortality. In the *Gathas* of the Seven Chapters the six cardinal attributes are called *Amesha Spenta*. As God is *spenta*, all his attributes are also *spenta*, holy. Zoroastrianism does not believe in pantheism, and nothing can be equated with God. *Ahura Mazda* is *Spenta Mainyu*, but *Spenta Mainyu* is not *Ahura Mazda*. Nothing but *Ahura Mazda* is God. Sun can provide an analogy. Through radiation sun gives light and heat; neither of the two is sun. *Spenta Mainyu* acts as a medium between the unchangeable celestial and changing terrestrial worlds, between the supersensuous and the sensuous. In the sensuous and the terrestrial world, *Spenta Mainyu* poses itself

---

[2] Zaehner, *The Dawn*, 45.

as the eternal antagonist of the evil and destructive forces. *Spenta Mainyu* is the foe of those who revolt against God and goodness. *Spenta Mainyu* is the idealization of a perfect life in this world. Falsification of the divine thought in creation leads to imperfection, destruction, and evil. *Spenta Mainyu* helps man to spread the love of *Vohu Mana* and protects the righteous against the incursion of evil thought.

Logos in the Judaeo-Christian tradition is compared to *Spenta Mainyu* in Zoroastrian tradition.[3] "Philo Judaeus unites the Greek and Jewish ideas about Logos and says that Logos is the first-born son of God and acts as viceregent of God in the world.[4] Logos also is creatively active and sometimes appears as God and other times as an attribute of God. Thus Logos and *Spenta Mainyu* share the three characteristics of creativity, father-son relationship with God, and viceregent of God in this world. They differ in that Logos is the first-born son of God, while *Spenta Mainyu*, as God's son, has always been with God; the first represents the idea of creation out of nothing and the latter a creation as old as God himself. (*Ahura Mazda* is Father of all his attributes.)

The distinction between *Spenta Mainyu* and *Ahura Mazda* fades out in *The Younger Avesta* and the Holy Spirit assimilates to God. Throughout the Avestan tradition *Spenta Mainyu* remains the essence of God's holiness. In this life man can attain self-realization, perfection, and happiness by following the Holy Spirit (*Spenta Mainyu*) and acting on holy mind and holy love.

> *Led by Thy* Holy Spirit *and Thy* love,
> *Led on by thoughts and words and deeds of* Truth,
> Perfect Eternal Life *shall man attain;*
> *Through* Khshatra *and through Holy Armaity,*
> *Mazda Ahura shall all these bestow.*
> (Gathas: Yasna 47–1)

---

[3] Duchesne-Guillemin, "The Western Response" 88; Waterhouse, 69; Zaehner, *The Dawn*, 106.
[4] Dhalla, *History*, 158.

Spenta Mainyu and Mysticism

Mysticism defies a precise definition. Commonly it suggests the perception of Ultimate Reality through personal spiritual experience, which holy individuals alone can undergo. Individuals led by the Holy Spirit (*Spenta Mainyu*), Bounteous Love (*Spenta Armaity*), and Good Mind (*Vohu Mana*) are holy.

Holiness in Zoroastrianism is synonymous with goodness, constructiveness, and bounteousness. Holiness does not result merely from practicing asceticism or constantly muttering prayers. Holiness is realized by a useful, benevolent, and active life.

Zoroastrian mysticism is explainable through holy wisdom, holy love, and holy justice. It is translatable into development and progress. Development and progress are used in both a quantitative and a qualitative sense. They imply a harmonious advancement that leads man toward self-realiztion and perfection.

The *Gathas* urge man to choose the Holy Spirit as his guide, to venerate and befriend him, and to seek his help in difficulties. Invocation of the Holy Spirit is always associated with good wisdom and bounteous love. In Zoroastrianism the perception of God is experienced through wisdom of conscience–illumination, which results from the merger of holy reasoning, morality, and holy love. Wisdom of conscience does not imply negation of sensory or rational methods. In the quest for God, reason and intuition, mind and conscience, unite and the seeker treads the path of truth.

Shahab-al-Din Sohravardi was a Muslim mystic philosopher of the thirteenth century who claimed he learned *Ishraq*–the discovery and realization of the Truth–from the teachings of Frashaoshtra and Jamaspa. The ancient sages of Iran combined intuition and reason, insight and logic, perception and reality *Kashf* and *Shohud* (discovery and unveiling), in their approach to Ultimate Reality. Recognition of the one path of *Asha* shows the moral dimension implicit in the process. The pursuance of the one path of *Asha* is of utmost importance to the mystics. Zoroastrian mystics know that only one path–the path of *Asha*–leads them to their goal. The *Gathas* warn man against falsehood. He who elects to act against the Holy Spirit, is a follower of *Druj*, falsehood. He is Ahriman, a foe of God.

Contrary to the biblical-koranic idea of a *creatio ex nihilo*, creation, according to Zoroastrianism, is materialized through

Spenta Mainyu, and it has always been with God. As a coworker with God, man's existence and qualities originate in God. The prospect of the experience of mystical union or direct communion with Ultimate Reality is forseen in the *Gathas*.[5] Zoroastrian mysticism does not transcend religious law, but exists within its precinct. In uniting with God, man does not vanish as a drop in the ocean. The ultimate process is a mystery and cannot be explained by finite words. It is the process of immortalization and return to the source. The closest analogy is that of reflection of light back toward the source for the righteous, and diffraction of light in the case of the wicked—the mirror consisting of man's deeds. Hence Zoroastrian mysticism is a "Mysticism of Infinity."[6]

Unlike *nous*, the concept postulated by the Greek philosopher Anaxagoras, *Spenta Mainyu* is not a quasi-independent spirit and does not act as an intermediary between the God and the world. It is a medium, not an intermediary. Nor is *Spenta Mainyu* identical with Plato's world-soul created by the Supreme Deity. *Spenta Mainyu* is only creatively active; it does not directly regulate the world. Regulation of the universe is *Asha*'s function. By rejecting *Spenta Mainyu*, man activates in his mind what is named *Angra Mainyu*. *Angra Mainyu* is the opposite of *Spenta Mainyu*. Thence the confrontation of *Spenta Mainyu* and *Angra Mainyu* commences as soon as man decides to act against *Spenta Mainyu*. It is an act of defiance against *Spenta Mainyu by* man. The mystics, by proceeding on the path of *Asha* toward perfection, relieve themselves of the temptation of opposing the *Spenta Mainyu*.

Mysticism is a strong feature of Zoroastrianism, and Zoroaster was the greatest mystic. Before receiving his mission, he saw God as a divine Person through theosophic contemplation; Zoroaster tried to establish a relationship with his newly perceived God. He saw God in his conscience; no physical meeting occurred. Zoroaster, through the Holy Spirit and Loving Wis-

---

[5] Equipped with the knowledge of Truth, *Yasna* 28-5, and through perpetual communion with Truth *Yasna* (31-21), one can achieve perfection and advance to the exalted presence of *Ahura Mazda Yasna* 34-3. Through Good Mind and Truth, and by supressing all anger, violence, ill-will and strife, benevolent persons can reach the presence of *Mazda yasnas* 48-7; 50-8.

[6] For a definition of the term and concept *see* Schimmel, 4-5.

dom, proceeded on the path of *Asha* toward the goal of Light.[7] It was the act of illumination. The Source of Light shed his rays of light on Zoroaster and he was illuminated. Zoroastrian mysticism is the theophilosophy of illumination.[8] The *Gathas*, unique for its aphorism, presents a God-centered world in which the Center is the sublime source of ontological and axiological perfection. Zoroaster's God is all positivity, constructiveness, and goodness. Zoroastrian mystical experience can be realized through holy meditation, constructive thinking, and positive actions. Negativity, idleness, and destruction removes man afar from mystical experience. Besides invocation of *Spenta Mainyu* and meditation through holy mind and love and the pursuance of *Asha*, no other mystic rituals are mentioned in the *Gathas*. Rites harmful to body and mind should be regarded as non-Zoroastrian.

Zoroaster declared that through emulation of God's attributes, man can have communion with God. It is communion with the qualities beyond time and space in infinity. Being an embodiment of holiness in this world, Zoroaster received the revelation of prophethood. Communion with God relates to man's will; it is open to every individual who becomes worthy of that experience. The granting of prophethood also relates to God's will.

The Zoroastrian concept of gnosticism originates in *Asha*. Self-realization and perfection are required for the experience of mystical union with God, and that can only be attained through emulation of God's manifested qualities. The six stages in procession toward perfection are the same as the six cardinal attributes of *Ahura Mazda*.

In Zoroastrian gnosticism, the starting point is a belief in: (1) God as the light of lights and as the quintessence of his attributes; (2) the doctrine that a gleam of God's attributes radiates in every human being, and (3) man can illumine that gleam within the self toward perfection by defying evil and following the path of truth, righteousness, and justice. The process of gnosticism consists of self-improvement in accordance with the law of *Asha*.

The strengthening of Good Mind, *Vohu Mana*, constitutes the first stage of gnosticism. Man must completely discard the bad mind, *Aka Mana*, and refrain from thinking evil. *Vohu Mana*, being the first creation–or to be more precise, the foremost ra-

---

[7] The *Gathas*; *Yasnas* 30-1,2; 31-20.
[8] Safa, 350.

diation of the Light of Lights–is closest to the Source. Nothing separates them; they are one. The light of *Vohu Mana* emanates from the source and disseminates light.

The second stage in gnosticism is the augmentation of right-eousness, *Asha*, which emanates from the light of Holy Mind. The triad of *Ahura Mazda*, *Vohu Mana*, and *Asha*, and the belief that all lights, including those of *Vohu Mana* and *Asha*, are re-flections of the Light of Lights of *Ahura Mazda*, are central to the Zoroastrian concept of gnosticism. The practice of *Asha* is not possible without a holy mind. It is through good (holy) rea-soning that an individual can discern between the goodness and badness of an act. In this stage strict observance of the truth is required; no white lie is permitted. The Islamic concept of *Taghieh*, or the expedient lie, is foreign to Zoroastrianism. Rec-titude of mind and piety of action invigorate the divine essence in the individual and help him to advance toward *Vahishta Mana*, the sublime and the universal mind–God's mind.

Perseverance in piety brings man nearer to the source, *Asha Vahishta*, the sublime and universal righteousness–God's justice. In this stage the individual acquires *Khshatra*, divine courage and power, which enables man to love and render selfless service to all fellow creatures. Through incessant altruistic service, an individual approaches *Khshatra Vairyo*, the sublime and univer-sal constructive power–God's power. From then on, man is in a position that cannot think or do evil. He is free from temptation, greed, desire, and rage. Thus man arrives at the threshold of the fourth stage–universal love, tranquility, and bountiful peace, *Spenta Armaity*. In this stage love for humanity replaces the in-dividual's love for himself, his family, and a small circle of friends; nepotism develops into universal brotherhood, which is a manifestation of love for God, or God's love.

The last two stages are those of perfection, *Haurvatat*, and immortality, *Ameretat*–communion with God. Perfection is syn-onymous with self-realization, and happiness in immortality is man's goal. The whole process reflects the unceasing struggle between *Spenta Mainyu* and *Angra Mainyu* discussed in this chapter.

It is commonly believed that Zoroastrian mysticism has influ-enced both Neo-Platonic gnosticism and Muslim Sufism.

Spenta Mainyu and Creation

In Zoroastrianism, creation approximates emanation. *Ahura Mazda* is *dadar* and designer, giver, and transformer. He radiates his bounties over all creation; creation emanates from him. The Zoroastrian idea of creation has influenced Islamic mysticism. Sohrevardi states that the essence is either light or darkness; the greatest is the Source of light–the Light of Lights, the Universal Light, beyond which nothing exists. According to Sohrevardi, only one Absolute Ray emanates from the Source and that is Intelligence or *Bahman* (*Vohu Mana*). Bahman is the most luminous and the closest to the Source. Other rays emanate from Bahman. The ninth ray in the hierarchy is the one that illumines the earth and the mind of man. In Sohrevardi's explanation, the rays of sun, moon, and fire are incidental to the Light of Lights; they are not essence.

In *Avesta*, the light that emanates from God and radiates man's mind is called *Xvarengha* or grace. By emulating *Spenta Mainyu* man can strengthen the *Xvarengha* within him and by opposing the Holy Spirit, cause the *Xvarengha* to leave him. In Iranian mythology, when King Yima followed falsehood, and by so doing turned against *Spenta Mainyu*, God's *Xvarengha* left him and he lost his kingdom.

Spenta Mainyu and *Angra Mainyu*

With the disappearance of the distinction between *Spenta Mainyu* and *Ahura Mazda* in *The Younger Avesta*, and by assimilation of the Holy Spirit to God, the way is paved for the substitution of the principle of cosmic dualism for that of ethical dualism. *Angra Mainyu*, the opposite of *Spenta Mainyu*, becomes Ahriman and assumes the position of the counterpart to Ohrmozd. *The Younger Avesta* speaks of good creations as belonging to *Spenta Mainyu* and evil creation to *Angra Mainyu*. At this stage the epic tradition of eastern Iran, mixed with pre-Zoroaster Indo-Iranian mythology, enters *Avesta* and supports the emergence of cosmic dualism. For instance, Azhi-Dahak, who deposed King Yima, is made into an Ahriman.

The doctrine of cosmic dualism in its pure form appeared in Manichaeanism in the third century and in Zurvanism in the fourth century A.D. Zurvanites viewed boundless time, *Zurvane Akarne*, as the origin and parent of the two opposite spirits of Ohrmozd (*Spenta Mainyu*) and Ahriman (*Angra Mainyu*). Another school that contributed to the dualist idea was Gayomartian of the fifth century A.D. The adherents of this school maintained that evil was derived from an unrighteous thought in the mind of Ahura, who once wondered whether it would be possible for him to have an opponent. Those were heretical schools.

For a Zoroastrian, evil is not a mystery. Evil is disobedience to *Ahura Mazda* and opposition to the Holy Spirit. Being created by *Ahura Mazda*, man belongs to him; being free to choose, man may turn against God and become destructive, wicked, and unholy. In this mental state, man is *Angra Mainyu*, of evil mind and of evil spirit. In order to remain the coworker and friend of God, man must remain virtuous. As already mentioned, virtue in Zoroastrianism is synonymous with fruitfulness, positivity, and constructiveness. Vice is sterility, destructiveness, and negativity. The Holy Spirit sets the example of the ideal life, which man must emulate. False religion is molested in its destructive results caused by deviation from the Holy Spirit's example.

Spenta Mainyu and *Angra Mainyu* represent the polarity between abundance and famine, augmentation and decrease, progression and regression, hope and despair. This moral duality can be traced to cosmic duality, which was a matter of faith for primitive man. Primitive man believed that both abundance and famine were caused by the forces of nature. Zoroaster changed pessimistic cosmic polarity into ethical and optimistic dualism. He declared evil to be a phenomenon resulting from man's actions; thus it could be forstalled by man.

To conclude, *Spenta Mainyu* is the manifestation of the creativity of *Ahura Mazda*; it is an aspect of God and it is not God; it has no existence independent of God and cannot be an intermediary between God and the world; it is the medium through which the goodness, holiness, and abundance of the unchangeable celestial world reveals itself in the changeable terrestrial world; it is the vehicle for the materialization of creation; it represents the ideal life in this world; in its worldly manifestation, it encounters the opposition force of those who disobey God and work for the destruction of the universe–the *Angra Mainyu*; it continues its struggle against evil forces until the attainment of the final triumph.

VI

IMMORTALITY OF THE SOUL

The Principle of Consequences and Divine Judgment

Those who are living, those who have been and those
who are yet to be,
Shall attain one of the two awards *which* He *ordained!*
In Immortality *shall the* soul of the Righteous *be*
ever in Joy,
But in torment the soul of the Liar *shall surely be.*
And these Laws *bath* Ahura Mazda *ordained through His*
sovereign authority.

(Gathas: Yasna 45–7)

Life after Death

Mazdaism believes in the survival of the soul (other existence in the other world) after bodily death and in the indispensable operation of the law of consequences. A corollary of the law of *Asha*, the law of consequences, is generally known as the principle of reward and punishment.

Since creation, man has wondered whence he came and whither he is destined! Answers to these questions require knowledge about oneself and the creator which Zoroaster gave us. He told us that God, who is Universal Wisdom and the Lord of Life, created us with an everlasting soul and faculties to discern between good and bad. He alerted us to the association of sustained happiness with goodness and of unceasing misery with wickedness. Zoroaster was the first to introduce divine judgment and an ethical dimension into life after death. The phenomenon of death, or nonlife, is a concept accompanying the advent of creation. According to the *Gathas*, at the dawn of creation, twin primal spirits manifested themselves; they were spontaneously active and through encounter with each other, established life and nonlife. So it shall be until the end of the world.

In his spiritual vision, Zoroaster conceived also of two kinds of existence and consequently two worlds, *Ahura*: spiritual, *Manahya*, and corporal, *Astavat*.[1] The *Gathas* are the first holy scripture with explicit reference to the hereafter. Buddhism believes in rebirth and the semi-eternity of being.[2] The Old Testament cursorily states that the dead dwell in the nether part of the earth.[3]

The concept of reward and punishment in the hereafter was first introduced by Zoroaster. Jews in the biblical period believed that the dead would continue to exist in a shadowy form, *Sheol*, in the lower part of the earth. After their encounter with Zoroastrianism in Babylon[4] or with socio-political oppression in the Greco-Roman world, the Jews gradually adopted the eschatological divine plan of salvation. The concept also appears in Christianity and in Islam.[5] In Christianity immortality is centered in the death–resurrection mystery of Jesus Christ. "The development within Jewish religion of such matters as ... eschatology and resurrection of the body is commonly attributed to the impact of Iranian religion."[6]

Eastern religions in their notion of matter and spirit and the concept of life after death differ drastically from Zoroastrianism and the Abrahamic religions. They generally believe in rebirth as a corollary of Karma. So long as the Karmic force–ignorance,

---

[1] *Yasna* 28-2.

[2] Although the reincarnation tenet is central to Karma dogma, the *Rig Veda* says nothing about it. According to *Veda,* the righteous would enter the heavenly world of the gods. Nothing is mentioned about the fate of the Wicked. The idea of reincarnation appears in the *Upanishads* of a later period. Young Oon Kim, *World Religions* vol. 2 San Francisco: Golden Gate Publishing Co., 49.

[3] The Old Testament, Psalms LXXXVIII: 12, CXV: 17; Job XIV: 2 1.

[4] Zaehner, *The Dawn*, 58; Duchesne-Guillemin, "The Western Response", 87.

[5] The closeness of the description of 'al-Sarat bridge', heaven and hell in Shia Islam with their counterparts in *The Younger Avesta* is striking.

[6] Barr, 201.

desire, and attachment (which are the root causes of life) – exists, the life process continues. Cessation of the life-stream constitutes the ideal, at which point the purified Self is Nirvanized and immortalized. Immortalization means merger in cosmic Nirvana. In this sense nonlife is the eternal. Zen speaks of Koan, which is a matter of one's life, the real life; when one dies Koan becomes one's true Koan and then life is really complete. Obviously the belief in life after death, or the life in death, is a matter of faith.

Despite differences in the basic concept of spirit and life, Zoroastrianism and Eastern religions resemble each other in one respect and that is belief in the law of consequences. In Hinduism, Buddhism and Sikism, Karma indicates that in each rebirth, the individual's current existence is determined by his previous existence. Every being inherits the Karma of past lives. The process of rebirth ceases when one reaches perfection. Being is not eternal but once the Atman, the true Self, is Nirvanized, it becomes immortal. The nature of Atman is not definable. It is self-awareness and the true Self. In Hinduism the subjective knowledge of the same reality, which is objectively known as Brahman, represents immortality.

In Zoroastrianism, *Asha* determines the consequences or fruits of an individual's acts and the fate of the soul after the individual's physical death. Physical death marks the end of one stage (one form of existence) and the beginning of a new stage in life (the other existence). The individual's acts in this world set the consequences into motion. One can condition and change one's future by changing one's actions. The individual's soul can reach self-realization and perfection, *Haurvatat*, through commitment to positive acts of love, devotion, and holy rationality; then it reaches immortality, *Ameretat*. In Buddhism, Karma means work and is translated into fate for the purpose of comparative religious studies; it is an individual's worldly work balance.

In Zoroastrianism, *Asha* is God's will. A Buddhist through refrainment from negative acts of desire, attachment, and ignorance can reach perfection, while a Zoroastrian can attain perfection only by positive acts. Refrainment from wickedness, though required, is not sufficient; positive and virtuously constructive deeds are required for salvation. *Asha* represents Justice and divine judgment in the hereafter regarding man's actions in this world. Justice is administered in the context of the causal law.

The Law of Consequences

The law of *Asha* denotes that every person receives his re-ward–the fruit of his action–Mizdem.[7] The reward of the evil-doer is not labeled retribution, retaliation, or punishment. It is the suffering that results from his consciousness of his alienation from *Ahura Mazda* in the life after death.[8]

Zoroastrian eschatology is noteworthy for its clarity, justice, and hope. Zoroastrianism is markedly spiritual. The *Gathas* speak of the two worlds: the corporeal, *Astvant*, and the spiritual, *Manahya*,[9] both of which are good. The *Gathas* speak of two principal constituents of man as body, *Tanu*, and soul, *Urvan*. This complementary dualism exists everywhere in creation. The universe has a cosmos, *Geush*, as well as a soul, *Geush Urvan*.[10] The soul continues its life after death. In this world the immortal soul exists along with the perishable flesh. The longer portion of an individual's existence is the life after death. After bodily death everyone's soul Joins the appropriate region of the spiritual world. The destination of the soul depends on the individual's life record.

The main features of Zoroastrian eschatology are:

1. The everlastingness of the soul: A human being does not perish completely after his or her visible worldly death. The body is annihilated but the soul survives.[11]

---

[7] The *Gathas; Yasna* 51-15. The word *Mizdem* in *Avesta* means reward.

[8] The *Gathas*; *Yasnas* 32-2; 9, 11; 33-8, 9. The wicked reside in darkness, uttering words of woe and regret, not being able to be in the abode of light. That sense of alienation would be the worst punishment.

[9] The *Gathas*; *Yasnas* 28-2; 43-3.

[10] The *Gathas*; *Yasna* 29-1.

[11] The *Gathas*; *Yasna* 45-7 "The soul of the righteous shall triumph in immortality; those of the sinners shall ever be in the renewed misery."

2. The causal law of consequences: An individual reaps what he or she sows. *Mizdem* means consequences and reward. Rewards or consequences automatically accrue to, or flow from, acts. The words *reward* and *punishment,* used freely in the translation of the word *Mizdem,* may be confusing. The consequences result from the operation of the law of *Asha. Ahura Mazda* stands beyond revenge, punishment, or anger; he is solely goodness. Consequences denote the accrued fruitions of one's acts. By their deeds in life, human beings earn those fruits.

3. The best existence for the righteous and the worst for the wicked: The nature and contents of consequences are described only in general terms in the *Gathas.* The soul of the righteous will lead a joyous life in the abode of the Best Existence and that of the wicked in the abode of the Worst Existence. Without recompense, the wicked will regret his worldly way of life. Heaven and hell are not physical places; they represent states of mental existence.

4. The life hereafter is the continuation of life in this world: the *Gathas* imply that the real nature of good life for the righteous, and bad life for the wicked, in the hereafter is the continuation of life in this world.

The *Gathas* alert human beings against deceptive, transitional, and ostensible victories that are illusory. The wicked will soon realize that his apparent victories have been failures in disguise.

> When on the False one destruction comes, and
> all his triumphs brought to naught by Truth,
> *From that time shall his mind retrace its steps;*
> His heart shall yearn to reach the blest abode
> *of* Mazda, Asha *and of* Vohu Mana,
> *Constantly striving to attain their grace.*
> (Gathas: Yasna 30–10)

The *Gathas* console righteous people not to be thwarted when they receive blows and condemnations from evil-doers in return for their good deeds. At the end, the evil-doers pay for their arrogance and injustice.

This I ask Thee, tell me truly,O Ahura!

He who will not give due recompense to the one
who well earns it,
Even unto the truthful man who fulfils his word
and work,
What penalty should he pay first here?
For, verily, I know well what he will get at the
last hereafter.

(Gathas: Yasna 44–19)

Consequences flow from one's actions in accordance with the law of *Asha.* It is the individual who, through his free choice, precipitates a predefined judgment. Therefore there is no predestined fate. The acts have predestined consequences. It is man's deeds that condition his life and future.

The Nature and Contents of Consequences

In life, human beings seek happiness and prosparity, *ushta*. Happiness originates in the law of *Asha. Asha* prescribes a life of joy, delight and prosparity for the pious and a life of eternal misery for the wicked.

O ye mortals, mark these commandments–
The commandments which the Wise Lord has given,
   for Happiness *and for* Pain;
Long suffering for the evil-doers, and bliss for the
   followers of Truth,
The joy of Salvation *for the Righteous ever afterwards*!

(Gathas: Yasna 30–11)

The *Gathas* do not specify particulars on the nature of consequences. Nor do they mention specific rewards or punishments.
It is essential to remember that in the *Gathas*, death is nonlife (*Ajyaiti*). Nonlife of body is the end of one stage of existence (*Gaya*) and the start of another. The other life is spiritual and by definition imperceptible to the senses. The righteous person should not fear death; nor should the relatives of the dead person mourn his or her departure. In the hereafter the righteous not

only is rewarded for his good deeds, but also is compensated for the ills he has suffered at the hands of evil-doers. *This constitutes the nucleus of martyrdom in Zoroastrianism.*

Persistent effort toward constructive change is a constant concern of Zoroastrianism. Improvement and refreshment of the world should be man's objective, and *Asha* will see that individuals working in that direction receive their right desert. The pious attain joy and happiness and the wicked suffer misery and dejection. Zoroastrians pray for a long life, happiness, and other boons for the purpose of promoting a blessed existence in this world and enjoying an unending happiness in the other world. The *Gathas* do not give details of life in the hereafter.

The reason for explaining consequences only in general terms is clear. Those consequences are spiritual rewards and punishments and thus are undefinable with finite concepts. At best they can be epitomized as the best and the worst existences. The finite terms are inadequate to define the nature of spiritual occurrences. However, the *Gathas* inform us that those consequences entail everlasting joy or woe. The deeds shall bear fruit; evil shall come to evil and good blessings to good.

> All thoughts and words and deeds *of men* shall bear
>   fruit *as laid down in Thine* Eternal Law,
> Evil to evil blessing good to good –
> *Thus wisdom thus ordained till end of time.*
>   (Gathas: Yasna 43–5)

The reckoning of the good and evil deeds of a person after death is effected before crossing to the other world.

The Crossing Boundary

The *Gathas* allude to *chinavat*, a dividing line or bridge between the two worlds (or the two existences). No particulars about the shape or locality of the bridge are provided. The term seems to have been used metaphorically indicating the end of one state of existence and the commencement of another. Or it may be a reference to the point of time when the final judgment is effected. The *Gathas* reveal that the judgment takes place at death and before crossing the dividing line. At that point the individual's life account in this world is compiled and closed.

> *I ask Ahura, that I learn from Thee,*
> *How the events have happened, and shall happen;*
> *What silenced yearnings of good men and true*
> *   have been recorded in the* Book of Life,
> *What yearnings, too, that follow the Untruth;*
> *How do these stand, when* the account is closed?
>   (Gathas: Yasna 31–14)

On that occasion pious souls will have an easy crossing; the prophet will be present, accompanying them to their destination. This, however, does not imply any mediation on the part of the prophet; the prophet's presence at the bridge is a matter of good leadership.

> *The man and woman, Mazda, who both bring,*
> *   to life what Thou hast as the best decreed, –*
> Asha's best blessing, Vohu Khshatra *named,*
> *The strength to serve, that comes through* Vohu Mana, –
> *All such I'll teach to* worship Thee and Thine
> *With them* I'll march *across* Thy Judgment Bridge.
>   (Gathas: Yasna 46–10)

Conversely, when crossing the bridge, the soul of the wicked will affect the prophet with grief and remorse.

> The False One *puts before his inner-self*
> *   a crooked picture of the path of Truth;*
> *But on the* Judgment-Bridge *his soul shall tax*
> *   him with his teaching false, this picture warped,*
> *Through* his own actions and his tongue untrue
> *   he goes astray, slipping from* Asha's path.
>   (Gathas: Yasna 51–13)

Furthermore, the *Gathas* reveal that the true selves, *Daenas*, of the wicked prick them and they will be assigned to the abode of lies. Other descriptions of the bridge and the scenarios mentioned in *Vendidad* (and later in Bundahishn and other Pahlavi works), should be taken as products of the creative imagination of their writers.

In an attempt to impress the simple and illiterate devotees, the authors of *Bundahishn* and *Arda Viraf Nameh* have dramatized the scenarios of hell and heaven to the point of absurdity. *Vendidad* which is obsessed with the usefulness and veneration of dogs, engages dogs at the entrance of the bridge, not as guards to bark away the wicked, but as guides to help the pious.[12] This pacifist function of dogs in the scenario is significant and may be referred to as an additional testimony to the non-aggressive nature of Mazdaism. The Pahlavi books enlarge the bridge-guards to include angels and spiritual dogs.[13] Among the angels that help the pious to cross the bridge are the two Yazatas, Sraosha, and Atar. But even in this context the Pahlavi books state that it is the conscience of the pious person that leads him to his destination.[14]

Without the piety which must originate in the soul, no Yazata can provide any help. The prolific imaginations of the Pahlavi writers do not stop here. They visualize a particular shape for the bridge and localize it in the space. Some of these speculations seem to have found their way into Islam.

Pahlavi books describe the bridge as a beam with many sides. Some sides are broad and others narrow. The bridge is so designed and its function so programmed that when a pious man is about to cross, the wide side presents itself and the pious passes easily. When a sinner is about to cross, the thin and sharp edge presents itself, hindering his passage.[15] It is also said that when the righteous soul wants to pass, the fire Frabag smites the darkness and the soul crosses over the sharp edge in the form of fire. Another development in Pahlavi writings is the assignment of a location to the bridge. The bridge is located in the middle of Iranevaeja and extends along and over the peak of Alburz Mountain. Of course these visually descriptive statements should not be taken seriously. In this area there is a marked difference between Gathic Zoroastrianism and post-Gathic tradition. In post-Gathic tradition some theologians have, for whatever reason,

---

[12] Vendidad, 19, 30.

[13] Bundahishn Modi, 5, 1, 7.

[14] *Dinkard*, vol. 2, 83.

[15] *Bundahishn Modi*, 10. Compare with Islam- in which the souls must cross the al-Sarat bridge. The al-Sarat bridge is finer than a hair and sharper than the edge of a sword; the soul of the wicked cannot cross it and falls into hell.

turned the abstract Gathic concepts into material and concrete descriptions.

Heaven: Abode of Good Mind, Song, Endless Light, and Good Existence

The *Gathas* state that the souls of righteous people in a state of perfect happiness go to the Abode of Song, *Garo Demana*; also called the Abode of Good Mind, *Vangheush Demana Manangho*. This place has no location in space. Destination of the soul, like the soul itself, is invisible and undefinable. In the *Gathas, Heaven and Hell are states of consciousness and not geographical regions.*

It was previously mentioned that a heavenly state is a continuation of the *Ashahya Gaetha*, the realm of righteousness, formed by Ashvan in this world. Put it differently, everybody is the maker of his/her own heaven. This confirms that in Mazdaism, heaven is a mental and spiritual state and not a physical location. The reward of the pious is felicity in immortality. It is a state without contradiction, without sorrow and evil; it is all bliss.

> *I shall take the soul to the* House of Songs, *with the help of the Good Mind*!
> *Knowing the* blissful rewards of Ahura Mazda *for righteous deeds,*
> *As long as I have power and strength, I shall teach all to seek for Truth and Right.*
>   (Gathas: Yasna 28–8)

This pure and non-material Gathic concept of a single heaven is transformed into a tangible and concrete fourfold heaven in *The Younger Avesta*, and a scenario for the welcoming reception of the pious souls is worked out. This scenario is further elaborated in the Pahlavi writings. Heaven is regionalized in the cosmos with sharp dividing lines between its different levels. Spiritual happiness assumes characteristics of worldly joy.

The *Garonmana* remains the highest stage and assumes also the name of Abode of Endless Light, *Anaghra Raochah*. The other three stages are called Good Thought, *Humata*; Good Words, *Hukhta*; and Good Deeds, *Hvarshta*. The ensemble of stages is called the Best Existence, *Vahishta Ahu*. In the highest heaven, *Garonmana*, resides *Ahura Mazda*, together with *Amesha Spentas*, *Yazatas*, and human souls that have reached perfection.[16] The arriving souls are fed with ambrosia by the *Fravashis* while they are being dressed by *Vohu Mana* in most luxurious clothes.[17] There the pious souls will enjoy everlasting happiness.

The Younger Avestan division of heaven is maintained in the Pahlavi books and is regionalized further; the good deeds of righteous people are quantified and each group, commensurate with its piety, is assigned to a division of heaven. The four heavens are located in a star region, a moon region, a sun region, and in a region called "The Endless Light." Heaven is exalted and described to be highly fragrant with sweet scented breezes and endless light. There the souls become radiant and beautiful. Dressed in embroidered and jewel-studded clothes, the souls sit on golden thrones. They walk on gold woven carpets, lean against reposeful cushions and are fed with spiritual food. According to the Pahlavi books, the state of felicity in heaven continues to the day of Resurrection.[18]

Regarding consequences, *Dadistan-i Dinik* advances a new interpretation of Gathic principles. It states that recompense or retribution is not based on the excess of good deeds over bad deeds or the reverse. The preponderance of good and bad determines the destination of the soul, not the process prior to it. Before arriving at the final destination, *Dadistan-i Dinik* maintains, the soul suffers retribution for each evil act and receives recompense for each good deed committed. Nobody can escape pain and suffering for the wrong he or she has committed. No trading of the good and bad in that process is allowed.[19] *Dadistan-i Dinik* argues that separate treatment of good and evil is the requirement of true justice. This shows that a difference in interpretation of Gathic principles existed even at the time of the composition of the Pahlavi books.

---

[16] Dhalla, *History*, 415.
[17] Ibid.5 416.
[18] Dadistan-i-Dinik, 31. 25.
[19] Dhalla, *History*, 419.

Hell: Abode of Wickedness, Worst Mind, Darkness, and Worst Existence

The destination of the wicked is the Abode of Wickedness, *Drujo Demana*, which is also called the Abode of Worst Mind, *Achishtahyā Demāna Manangho*, and Worst Existence, *Achishta Ahu*.

No physical torture is mentioned as retribution; the *Gathas* say that the impious will suffer unhappiness, misery, and grief. It is only in *The Younger Avesta* that the retributions are materialized.

> *But who deceiveth the good and the righteous,*
> *For him shall be the future* long life of misery *and*
>   darkness, woe and despair,
> *O ye men of evil lives! Your own deeds shall lead*
>   *you to this dark existence.*
> (Gathas: Yasna 31–20)

Hell has no location in Gathic Mazdaism; it is only associated with darkness and misery. How long will the soul of an impious person suffer misery? According to the *Gathas*, it would suffer a long time[20] till the Light Divine and Iluumination of Salvation dawn upon them.[21]

Like heaven, hell turns into a fourfold division establishment in *The Younger Avesta*. The divisions are called Evil Thought, *Dushmata*; Evil Word, *Dushhukhta*; Evil Deed, *Dushhavarshta*; and Endless Darkness, *Anaghra Temah*. The divisions of the ensemble are designated as the Worst Existence, *Achishta Ahu*, and the Evil Existence, *Duzh Ahu*. In hell impious souls are entertained with poisonous and foul food.[22] On entering hell, the impious souls tremble with fear. Thus the first step toward materialization of hell was taken in *The Younger Avesta*.

In the Pahlavi books, the four divisions of the Worst Existence are maintained and geographically localized. They are situated in the middle of the earth, below the Chinavat Bridge.[23] Hell is described as a deep, dark, cold, filthy, and dreadful place. The

---

[20] The *Gathas*; *Yasnas* 31-20; 46-11.
[21] The *Gathas*; *Yasna* 30-11.
[22] Dhalla, *History*, 287.
[23] Bundahishn, 12.7.

place is infested with noxious creatures and inhabited by de-mons. In the middle of hell runs a river filled with the tears of human beings. At the entry the sinful souls are met by demons. The sinful souls are then chained and physically tortured. The sinful souls cry and moan and are treated with scorn and mock-ery by Ahriman. The souls are punished by the very demons who have misled them in the worldly life. The physical tortures men-tioned in *Ardi Viraf Nameh* show the imaginative ability of the writer in matching the spiritual punishments to the worldly tor-ments.[24]

The Pahlavi book of Bundahlshn says that *Mashya* and *Mashyoi*, the mythical first human beings, corresponding to Adam and Eve in Abrahamic religions, were sent to hell because they lied to *Ahura Mazda* and acted in breach of the divine order. To what extent interaction between Zoroastrianism and the Judaeo-Christian tradition is responsible for the incorporation of this idea in Bundahishn is hard to say. Bundahishn also states that someone who converts from the Zoroastrian faith to other religions will go to hell.

The duration of suffering in hell is not specified. Some pas-sages allude to its permanence and others to a time of resurrec-tion or refreshment of the world.

An Intermediary Place

The principle stated and explored in the *Gathas* is that of pre-cise reward for all one's actions. The reward is happiness or mis-ery. Anything beyond that would be speculation an attempt to explain abstract and infinite ideas in finite and concrete terms. The *Gathas* do not address such details. *The Younger Avesta* embarks on greater details concerning life after death and speaks also of a place between heaven and hell, where the souls with an equal record of good and evil reside. That place is called *Mis-vana Gatu*, the place of mixing. No description of that place and

---

[24] The story of *Arda Viraf* who makes a trip to heaven under the effect of narcotics, might have been the source for the *Divine Comedy* of Dante.

no explanation of the nature of reward and punishment therein is provided in *The Younger Avesta.*[25]

In its distinctive manner of presentation, *Vendidad* localizes the intermediary place now called *Hamistagan* between the earth and the starry region.[26] An account of the conditions at Hamistagan is very scanty. Its climatic conditions are very much like those on earth: hot in summer and cold in winter. Beyond that they are not exposed to any hardship or mental agony. These people continue to live in a mental world (which they themselves form) similar to that of this world; their state of being is the continuation of their worldly existence. This situation continues until the day of refreshment of the world.

Transition from this World to the Other World

The Younger Avesta gives an account of the transition from this world to the other world that explains the rationale for the ceremonies performed on the occasion of someone's death. According to that account, the soul of the dead person does not leave his body at once. It takes three days and nights before complete separation occurs. During this period the soul stays near the place where the head of the dead was resting immediately before death. This reaffirms the closeness, if not the identity, of mind and spirit in the Zoroastrian tradition. The soul stays there during that period, recounting all the acts it has done in its life. If the soul has been righteous, it would "spend his time chanting the sacred hymns, and experiencing as much joy as the whole of the living world can experience collectively."[27] He anxiously would be waiting for the fruits of his deeds in the hereafter. In contrast the wicked soul will be sitting next to his skull, recalling his evil acts in a state of confusion and awaiting the terrible consequences of his action. During that period he "experiences as much suffering as the whole of the living world can experience collectively."[28] (It is interesting to note that the

---

[25] Dhalla, *History*, 286.

[26] Vendidad, 7, 52.

[27] Dhalla, *History*, 416.

[28] Dadistan-i-Dinik, 16.4.

Jews also believed that the soul fluttered in the neighborhood of his/her house for three days.)

For the first three days and nights, the soul associates with his "mind," recalling all he has done through the council of his mind. On the dawn of the fourth day, he starts his journey to the next world. At the bridge he is met with his *daena*. The *daena* of the righteous person appears in the shape of a beautiful maiden and takes the person's soul toward the Abode of Good Mind. On the way, the righteous soul inhales the most refreshing sweet-scented air. In contrast, the sinner is met by the personification of his conscience in the shape of an ugly woman.[29] J. H. Moulton's verse translation of the relevant *Yasht* beautifully depicts this scene:

> Four glorious dawns had risen,
> And with the wakening loveliness of day
> Came breezes whispering from the southern sky,
> Laden with fragrant sweetness. I beheld,
> And floating lightly on the enamored winds
> A Presence sped and hovered over me,
> A Maiden, roseate as the blush of morn
> Stately and pure as heaven, and on her face
> The freshness of a bloom untouched of time.
> Amazed, I cried, "Who art thou, Maiden fair,
> Fairer than aught on earth these eyes have seen?"
> And she in answer spake, I am Thyself,
> Thy thoughts, thy words, thy actions, glorified
> By every conquest over base desire,
> By every offering of a holy prayer
> To the Wise Lord in Heaven, every deed
> Of kindly help done to the good and pure.
> By these I came thus lovely, came to guide
> Thy steps to the dread bridge where waits for thee
> The prophet, charged with judgment.

The third component that continues operation after death is the *Fravashi*. On the fourth day after death, the *Fravashi* of the departed is invoked together with the *Fravashis* of all righteous people. The *Fravashis* of the righteous people, not of sinners, visit the world regularly on special days. The Farvardingan ceremony in the month of March and the five days at the end of

---

[29] *Dinkard*, vol. 2, 83.

the Zoroastrian calendar year are dedicated to the *Fravashis* of the dead, which are invoked and adored by their relatives and all righteous people. Remembrance ceremonies are performed on the tenth day following the death, thereafter on each 30th day of the month for one year and finally annually for thirty years.

To conclude, Mazdaism believes in the continuation of existence in the hereafter; in everlasting happiness for those righteous people who helped to refresh the world; in long-lasting suffering for those who, with an evil mind, hindered the progress of the world; in the hereafter life as a continuation of the conditions each individual has opted for himself or herself; and in final divine judgment.

> *With my songs of praise, with my self-humbling*
>   *worship I wish to serve my Lord*!
> *For now, indeed, I see Him with my own eyes, the*
>   *Lord of Good Spirit, the Lord of Good Word and Deed*
> *I know Him through Truth, who is* Ahura Mazda!
> *Verily, I shall render Him my homage* in the House of Songs.
>   (Gathas: Yasna 45–8)

VII

FRASHO-KERETI:
REFRESHMENT

The Principle of the Final Triumph of Goodness

So may we be like those making the world refresh
    towards perfection;
May Ahura Mazda *help us and guide our*
efforts through   Truth;
For a thinking man is where Wisdom is at home.

               (Gathas: Yasna 30–9)

Refreshment of the World

Is there an end to the constructive, progressive, and evolutionary movement of creation? What does the law of *Asha* pre-
scribe?

There is no end to creation; *Ahura Mazda* is eternal and creation is everlasting. Likewise, there is no end to the law of *Asha.*
Righteousness persists and the law of *Asha* remains immutable.

The *Gathas,* however, refer to "the End of Time." What is the
end of time? The end of time is a Great Turning Point–an occur-
rence that marks the attainment of a noble goal by a righteous
man. The righteous, through individual and collective efforts,
look to that event–renewal of the world and establishment of a
new order, (what in Christianity is known as the establishment of
God's kingdom on earth.)[1] That event will mark the end of one
stage and the start of a new one in the history of mankind. The
turning point is the culmination of a long process of gradual pro-

---

[1] The *Gathas*; *Yasna* 30-9; 34-15; *Yasna* 43-4, 5, 6, 9, 10 concerns
God's judgment, the goal of creation, destiny, and reward.

gress–both quantitative and qualitative–toward perfection. Perfection (self-realization) and immortalization (*Haurvatat* and *Ameretat*) are the goal and hope of true Mazdayasnan. "Refreshment of the world" is the result of the accumulation of the individual and collective acts of *Ashvan*; it is characterized by a new order universal harmony, goodness, and happiness. *Haurvatat* qualifies the individual to join the Abode of Endless Light and to attain the best existence; collective *Haurvatat* turns the whole world into the Abode of Endless Light. Refreshment, *Frasho-Kereti*, or "renovation of the world," as it is called in Christianity, is the ideal end; that end will be realized because it is *Ahura Mazda*'s will. The time of arrival of the new stage depends on the nature and intensity of man's holy (constructive) endeavors, which are motivated by good thought. The inescapable triumph of good over evil is one aspect of *Ahura Mazda*'s omnipotence. That omnipotence constitutes divine *Khshatra*, good's hegemony, on earth. All this is conceived in God's *Vahishta Mana*, the Universal Intelligence.

Thus, "refreshment" refers to the final destination of the collective efforts of the righteous people, *Ashvans*, at one phase of existence. It is regeneration of the existence. It is the end of disharmony, contradiction, struggle, and discomfort; it proclaims the consummation of accord, peace, and love. It is the end of relativity and time and the beginning of timelessness. The refreshed state represents absoluteness, oneness, and unity. It marks the end of the finite. The word *refreshment* connotes infinity, immortality, and eternity.

> *Whatever words and deeds are noblest, best,*
> *teach me, O Mazda, make my life express,*
> *Through Love of Fellow-man, through search for Truth,*
> *the yearnings and the prayers of my heart;*
> Refresh, *Ahura, through the Strength to Service,*
> *my life, and make it as Thou wishest–True.*
> (Gathas: Yasna 34–15)

To refresh means to regenerate and renew. Refreshment of the world heralds regeneration of the creation and infallibility of man. It is not destruction of one state and construction of another. It is the apex of the perfection of the existing world in its evolutionary process.

The components of the Gathic refreshment of the world are: the gradualness of the process, the joint contribution of righteous people, and the divine judgment. Distortion of some of these components, particularly the personality of *Saoshyant* in the later Zoroastrian tradition, is noteworthy.

Gradualness denotes the absence of abruptness in the change at the turning point. It is a continuous change through persistent mental and physical purification, spiritual uplifting, development, and augmentation. In this process *Spenta Mainyu*, *Ashvans*, and *Saoshyants* are at work.

Saoshyant

The Gathic *Saoshyant* is not a particular individual. In the holy book *Saoshyant* is used in a generic sense, meaning "a group of saintly workers."[2] Thus in Gathic Mazdaism numerous saviors are forseen; they do not appear or act at set intervals but exist and operate in all times. In this sense *Saoshyants* are not of the same rank in righteousness, and the role they play in the perfection of the world differs. Ceaseless and selfless service can promote an *Ashvu* in his own right to the position of a *saoshyant*. *Saosbyants* are observers of the Law of *Asha*, preachers of truth, and promoters of justice by deeds. The continuous contribution of righteous people–including the prophet, *Ashvans*, and *saoshyants*–brings about the refreshment of the world. This idea is clearly set out in the following two Gathic passages. The first passage speaks of those who abide by the commandments of *Ahura Mazda* and stand against falsehood; the second passage identifies those persons as *saoshyants*, the saviors of earth.

> When *will Armaity come and* Asha, *too,*
>   rewarding Services, bringing Peace and Rest?
> *When bloody tyrants, following Untruth,*
>   *rush in from every side, who'll stand erect,*

---

[2] The *Gathas*; *Yasna* 45-11 (saviour, *Saoshyant*). In the *Gathas* the term *Saoshyant* is used in a generic sense, both in singular and plural. *See* Dhalla, *History*, 108.

and upright, firm in Vohu Mana's *Love?*
(Gathas: Yasna 48–11)

Such is indeed, the Saviors of the Earth
They follow Duty's call, the call of Love:
Mazda, they listen unto Vohu Mana;
They do wkat Asha *bids, and Thy Commands*;
Surely they are the vanquishers of Hate.
(Gathas: Yasna 48–12)

Another passage reveals that *Ahura Mazda* will protect and befriend those who oppose the evil-doers (*Daevas*). According to the *Gathas*, such persons are saviors. This is ordained in the law of *Asha*.

He who denies the Daevas and their men
   as they deny Him, who is Lord of All,
   as they oppose Him in each thought and deed;
Who so obeys and pays Him reverence
   is Savior, *Lord of Wisdom, –he reveals,*
O Mazda Ahura, the Path of Life, –
Our friend, our brother, father he becomes.
(Gathas: Yasna 45–11)

The prophet is the Savior *par excellence-the* Chosen Savior.

My Lord, when shall the day dawn for winning
   the world to the cause of Truth?
When shall the wise Spiritual Guides *come with*
   the sublime teachings of Thy Chosen Saviour?
To the help of whom shall they come with the
   Good Mind?
As for me, I have chosen Thee as my instructor,
   Ahura Mazda.
(Gathas: Yasna 46–3)

In the Old Testament, too, Messiah is not used to designate an individual savior. The word is employed thirty-nine times, none of which has Messianic connotation. Among them are Cyrus, the king of Iran (Isaiah 45:1); the kings of Israel and the High Priest (Daniel 9:25–26 and Leviticus 4:3, 6:22). The term *Messiah* means "anointed" or "consecrated." This concept is in line with the Gathic *Saoshyant*. The two biblical Messiahs of ben Joseph and ben David of Judaism come later, as do the three *Saoshyants* of the Avestan tradition.

The Greeks knew of the Zoroastrian–or as they called it, the Magian–concept of renovation of the universe and of the collective judgment of souls.[3] The process of renovation changed in *The Younger Avestan* and Pahlavi traditions, though its gradualness remained intact. The gradualness differentiates Zoroastrianism from these other religions (for instance, Islam), that expect the appearance of the savior at a time when the world is replete with injustice and rage and the savior comes to eliminate evil and establish God's kingdom on earth.

The striking difference between the *Gathas* and *The Younger Avesta* in the area of refreshment relates to the personality of the Savior. In *The Younger Avesta* three distinct saviors emerge: *Ukhshyat-ereta; Ukhshyat-nemah* and *Astvat-ereta*. An extraordinary mythical story is related to their birth. They will be born from virgin mothers and are from Zoroaster's descent. According to Farvardin Yasht, the last and most effective *Saoshyant*, Astvat-ereta will be conceived by a virgin called *Vispataurvi*, meaning "the all-triumphant." Zoroaster's seed is in the Hamun lake and is watched over by ninety-nine thousand nine hundred and ninety-nine *Fravashis*.[4]

Zoroaster's doctrine of refreshment must have greatly attracted the Greeks. Plutarch wrote that the Magians (Zoroastrians) believe that upon the "renovation" of the world, mankind will speak one language and have one commonwealth; men will live without food and they will not cast shadows.[5]

Pahlavi works elaborate on the Avestan doctrine and add ramifications to it, including the ascription of a time cycle to it. One of the Pahlavi books states that the prophet in a dream or vision sees a tree with several branches in gold, silver, and iron, each of which represented an era!

While retaining the Gathic gradualness of the process of refreshment and the final triumph of good over evil, the Pahlavi books have added new features to it. The new features include that of the appearance of distinct *saoshyants* with supernatural birth incidents at regular intervals; physical resurrection of all

---

[3] Haug, 5, 312.
[4] *Yashts* 13-62, 128, 129, 142; 19-22, 95, 89.
[5] Dhalla, *History*, 290.

the dead and universal judgment; devilization of the most hei-
nous sinners, and purification of the other sinners.

According to the later Zoroastrian tradition, Gayomart, Jamshid, and Zoroaster were the saviors. Gayomart was the mythological archetypal man whose seed had passed into the earth; and
therefrom the first human couple grew. Jamshid or Yima was the
ideal prototype of kings. He ruled with justice and constructed a
cavern, a *vara*, at God's order, before the Ice Age. In that cavern
Yima kept the best human beings, the seeds of all animals and
plants during the Three Terrible Cold Winters (similar to the
Semitic story of Noah and the Flood). On the other hand, Yima
is condemned by Zoroaster for falsehood. He had given ox flesh
to men to eat and had lied by claiming divine qualities.

At the time of the appearance of *Saoshyant*, mankind will be
greatly advanced through righteousness; under the guidance of
spiritual leaders, hunger and thirst, disease and poverty, rage and
ruthlessness will be largely eliminated. *Saoshyant* comes to give
the final touch to the perfected work and to bring about the final
victory.

Pahlavi writers assert that the three *Saoshyants* will come in
the last three millenia before the end of the world, at regular intervals, each at the end of a millenium. The first millenium belongs to *Hoshidar*, which is the Persian word for the Avestan
Ukhshyat-ereta. The second millenium is that of *Hoshidar mah*,
the Persian rendering of the Avestan *Ukhshyat-nemah*. The third
or the last one is *Soshyos*, the *Saoshyant* proper.

They all have supernatural birth and are of *Zoroaster's descent*. The Muslim Shi'a, unlike the Muslim Sunni, believe that
the twelfth Imam who is of *Ali's* descent will reappear as *Mahdi*
or Savior. The three *Saoshyants* will miraculously be born from
virgin mothers. According to this account, on three occasions
when Zoroaster went to his wife, *Hvovi*, his seed went toward
the ground and was caught by *Yazata Nairosangha* (*Neryosangin*
in Pahlavi), the divinity of fire, who entrusted it to *Yazata Ardva
Sura Anahita*, the divinity of water, who placed it in the lake
Kans.[6] The seed remained in Lake Kans until the appointed time.
On each occasion a fifteen-year-old virgin girl approached the
water and by drinking or bathing in it, became pregnant. The
names of the virgin girls were given as *Shemik-abu, Shapir-abu*,

---

[6] *Dinkard*, vol. 47, 7.10.8. 114; *Bundahishn*, 30.1; Dhalla, *History*, 426.

and *Gobak-abu*. According to Zoroastrian tradition, the *sa-oshyanta* will be conceived on the day of Norooz (at the time of the spring equinox); according to the Shi'a tradition, the twelfth Imam will reappear on the Norooz day.[7]

Certain miracles are also associated with those supernatural births. At the age of thirty, the three *Saoshyants* hold a conference with Ormazd (the Pahlavi rendering of *Ahura Mazda*), on which occasions they receive revelations. On their return to earth, they exhibit the miraculous act of making the sun stand still in order to convince people of their divine mission. Hoshidar's miracle lasts for ten days, Hoshidamah's for twenty, and Soshyos' for thirty days.[8] While Zoroaster had no claim to supernatural power or to any miracle, how can miracles for *Saoshyants* be justified?

Physical resurrection is peculiar to Pahlavi tradition. The *Gathas*, or *Avesta*, do not recognize it. This is abundantly clear in Bundahishn, where it is stated that Zoroaster himself had doubted the physical resurrection. According to Bundahishn, the prophet had exclaimed that with the disintegration of the body and the destruction of matter, the reconstruction of the body would not be possible. In response to the prophet, Bundahishn says, Ohrmozd declared that he who created the universe out of nothing, was able to resurrect, to form anew, something that had already existed.[9] *Dadistan-i Dinik*, in support of this view, reasons that as it is easier to repair a building than to construct a new one, it is easier for God to restore the creation as it was than to make something new.[10] From these argumentations, one can infer that the idea of physical resurrection was so controversial that the author of Bundahishn had to resort to incredible stories, in order to lend credibility to the concept. Dinkard maintains that the bodies of the most repulsive criminals, such as sodomites and apostates, will not resurrect, whereas *Dadistan* states that everybody, righteous or wicked, will resurrect in his or her bodily shape. The physical resurrection will start with Gayomart,

---

[7] According to Islam, *Mahdi* (Messiah) appears when the world is replete with injustice, corruption, vice, tyranny, and godlessness (the logical inference is that the human beings are on a decline); in Zoroastrianism the world is progressing and moving towards righteousness.

[8] *Yasht* 19; *Bundahishn*, 32.8.

[9] *Bundahishn*, 70-71; Haug, 373.

[10] *Dadistan, Dinik*, 375.

Mashya, and Mashyoi. Some mythological and folkloric names are also added that give the book a legendary rather than a theological air.[11]

The next stage is the process of universal or collective judgment by Ormazd. All human souls, from Gayomart to *Saoshyant*, receive the final judgment. The assembly also serves as a reunion place for relatives and friends. In this scenario, the righteous cry for the suffering of their wicked relatives and friends; the wicked complain that the righteous did not sufficiently warn them against evil-doings. The moral message of this scenario is clear. It emphasizes man's duty to guide others. After the final judgment the righteous souls are separated and sent back to heaven in order to enjoy the best existence; the sinners are sent back to hell to receive physical punishment. The physical punishment lasts three days. According to these accounts, the wicked incur physical and mental sufferings in this world, mental sufferings in hell after being judged individually, and again physical punishment during the three days after the universal judgment. Some Pahlavi writings say that criminals like Afrasiab and Zohak, because of their grave sins, will be made into the form of the devil; after the decisive victory of good over evil they will be completely destroyed and eliminated. Other Pahlavi writers favor the view that all sinners, having received the requisite punishment, will be redeemed.[12]

The last episode in the Pahlavi scenario of renovation is the flow of a boiling flood of the metals of *Shatravan*. The righteous and the wicked have to cross it. The righteous souls will not even feel the heat. The wicked souls will be purged of their sins and thus will be wholly purified.[13] Thereafter the purified souls will be released from hell and led into heaven, where they will join their virtuous relatives and friends. There they will enjoy happiness and eternal joy but, undoubtedly because of their sufferings in hell and in the three days after the universal judgment, their joy cannot be as profound as that of the originally virtuous persons.

The last item on the agenda is the destruction of demons. The presentation of renovation in the Pahlavi books is sensational

---

[11] Dhalla, *History*, 427, 428.

[12] Dinkard, vol. 2 104; vol. 8, 476.

[13] *Bundahishn*, 30-18, 19, 20.

and as such has attracted the attention of many researchers. The mystery of death and immortality constitutes an essential feature of all religions that believe in some sort of immortality. The majority of them consider death to be the annihilation of the body and the beginning of a new life. Physical death is the gateway to a different form of existence. All believe in the final purification of the soul, or consciousness, either through a cycle of death–rebirth, or by undergoing sufferings in the hereafter for the sins committed. They differ in their accounts of the nature of suffering and physical resurrection. The question of death–resurrection is the core of Christianity. Bodily resurrection is not mentioned in the *Gathas*; it developed in Pahlavi Zoroastrianism, as did the description of the nature of the punishments. Islamic eschatology, like Zoroastrian Pahlavi writings, gives a colorful description of the punishments in the grave and in hell. The inclusion of legendary and mythical personages in the scenarios of resurrection in Pahlavi books reveals their mixed legendary-theological nature. Admittedly they may serve some good moral purpose for illiterate devotees. Their moral adages can be employed usefully in the propagation of truth and righteousness. Nevertheless, it is important to realize that they are not of Gathic origin.

The *Gathas* talk of the "divine fire" being used as the test on the day of judgment; this divine fire should not be taken as the physical fiery test. It is the fire that brightly shines in the heart of every righteous Zoroastrian. In Zoroastrianism, God is the eternal light; light is the very nature of God. In the words of Dastur Dhalla, "Light in its various manifestations, whether as the fire of the hearth on earth, or as the genial glow of the sun in the azure vault of heaven, or the silvery sheen of the crescent moon in the sky, or the flickering brilliance of the stars in the firmament, or even in the form of life-giving energy distributed unto the entire creation, is emblematic of Mazda. No wonder, then, if the prophet of Ancient Iran made fire the consecrated symbol of his religion, a symbol which in point of sublimity, grandeur, and purity, or in its being the nearest earthly image of the heavenly Lord, is unequalled by any of its kind in the world."[14]

Reference to the test of divine fire is no more than the test of the law of *Asha*, which lays bare the record of man's deeds. Fur-

---

[14] Dhalla, *History*, 63.

thermore, it is the law of *Asha* that determines the nature of reward.

> *Both parties, True and False, are put to test,*
>   *O Mazda, by blazing* Fire Divine,
> *This Fiery Test* lays bare their inmost Souls,
>   *as the* award *to each one indicates*;
> *Complete frustration shall the* False One *find*,
>   *the* blessing full *the* Truthful One *shall reap.*
>   (Gathas: Yasna 51–9)

The physical fire burns; it does not give frustration to the
wicked and joy to the virtuous–what this stanza says it does. The
only conclusion, therefore, is that the word *fire*, in this and other
stanzas related to the final reward and punishment, is used metaphorically and should be construed as divine fire. The prophet
declares that as love (*Armaity*) and justice (*Asha*) grow within
the seekers of Truth, they will be directed on the path of *Asha*
and the *Divine Fire* of *Wisdom* will give them their reward.

> *By this Bountiful spirit of Thine, O Mazda*
> *And through Thy Holy Fire,*
> *Thou shalt apportion good and evil to the two*
>   *contending parties,*
> *With Truth and Right-minded justice standing by*
>   *Thy side,*
> *Verily, this shall cause many to hear Thy Message.*
>   (Gathas: Yasna 47–6)

The might of the divine fire is in *Truth*, and not in its confla-
gration.

> *Verily I regard Thee as the Holy and Powerful*
>   *Benefactor, O Mazda.*
> *For Thou bestoweth upon the righteous as well as*
>   *the wicked their recompense,*
> *From the flaming splendour of Thy Fire, mighty*
>   *through Asha (Truth),*
> *The power of the Good Mind comes to me, O Mazda.*
>   (Gathas: Yasna 43–4)

The *Gathas* are replete with references to the "spiritual fire,"
Mainyo Athracha, and to the "inner fire."

Who hears the Truth and lives it in his life,
  soul-healing Lord of Wisdom he becomes;
  To spread true teachings, Ahura, his words
  are eloquent and able to convince;
O Mazda, through Thy Fire blazing clear,
  unto each man his place do the assign.
                            (Gathas: Yasna 31–9)

Fire in Zoroastrianism, as in other traditions, symbolically represents God. In the New Testament it is stated that "Our God is a consummate fire"[15] and in Islam, God (Allah) is the light of the sky and earth.[16] In Sinaitic revelation, God (Yahweh) "descended upon Mount Sinai in fire; and the smoke thereof ascended as the smoke of a furnace, and the whole mountain quaked greatly."[17] The blazing fire in the above passages in the *Gathas* refers to the inevitable consequences of one's deeds as a result of God's law of *Asha*. It is not a reference to the suffering or punishment of the wicked alone; it points to bliss and happiness too. The bliss and the suffering that result from the law of *Asha* are disclosed in the light of God's inner fire:

What Thou hast through Thy Inner Fire *disclosed,*
  the bliss through Asha *promised to us all,*
  the Law Divine for the discerning soul;
All that to us, O Mazda, clear explain,
  in words of aspiration from Thy mouth,
  to help us to convert all living men.
                            (Gathas: Yasna 31–3)

The *Gathas* and Reincamation

The idea of reincarnation does not exist in the *Gathas*. A return to this worldly existence in order to atone for one's sins is nowhere mentioned in the *Avesta*. In reverse, the idea of reward and punishment in the hereafter is explicitly referred to in the

---

[15] The New Testament: Hebrews, xii, 29.
[16] Koran: Light, 35.
[17] The Old Testament: Exodus xix, 17, 18, 19, 20.

Gathas. Any suggestion regarding reincarnation in Zoroastrianism, therefore, must be rejected for lack of evidence.

The Final Triumph of Good

The *Gathas* promise the final triumph of good over evil. The *Gathas* speak about the "end," which means the end of the first phase of creation. Belief in the "end" and the coming of the Messiah is ingrained in the followers of Zoroastrianism, Judaeo-Christian and Shi'a-Islam traditions. However, unlike the *Gathas*, the origin of the Messianic belief in the Jewish sources is obscure. It is suggested that the idea of *Aharith ha-Yamin* or the End of the Days of Isaiah and Daniel was influenced by the idea of Zoroaster. The Gathic idea of the last day triumph of good persists in *The Younger Avesta*. But the Pahlavi books, in an attempt to complete the personification of the Ahriman, end the projected account with a final battle between *Amesha Spentas* and *Yazatas* on the one hand and their devilish counterparts on the other. Having smitten the evil forces, the beings from the good forces become united and enjoy an existence devoid of conflict. All human beings will be united in good thought, word, and deed. There will be no disharmony, contradiction, and struggle. Living in union with *Ahura Mazda*, all human beings in their new existence will praise and extol *Ahura Mazda*'s glory.

To conclude, Zoroastrianism is the religion of action, justice, and hope. Active life means righteous life; justice is secured by insuring that each individual reaps what he or she sows; hope is inculcated in man by immortality and best existence in the hereafter. There is no end to life; there are different stages in existence. Conscious of the final triumph of good over evil, man in all stages of life should consult good mind (Vohu Mana), pursue righteousness (*Asha*) and serve mankind with love (*Armaity*) in order to achieve perfection (*Haurvatat*) and immortality (*Ameretat*). The goal is *Ushta* (happiness) and *Vahishta Ahu* (the best existence).

> *At the last turning of life,*
> *To the faithful making the right choice according to*
> *His norm,*

Doth Ahura Mazda, the Lord judge, in His
      sovereign Power,
Bestow an end better than good.
But to him who shall not serve the cause of good
He giveth an end worse than bad.
At the last turning of life.

(Gathas: Yasna 51–6)

EPILOG

This book presents the Gathic principles-the perennial tenets of Zoroastrian religious traditions. Originally a divine message, the Zoroastrian religion in its long history has been used to serve a variety of socio-political needs in changing societies and at times has functioned variously as a moralizer, liberator, nationalizer, and legitimizer. Its tenets have been interpreted differently by the oppressors and the oppressed.

The Gathic principles are embedded in the *Gathas*; they have been reincorporated, reinterpreted, modified, and distorted in the Avestan and Pahlavi writings. Consequently several traditions have emerged; and this book is concerned only with the Gathic tradition and principles. The Gathic principles have survived the vicissitudes of history and are still practiced by Zoroastrians, and as such they constitute the perennial tenets of the faith revered by Zoroastrians the world over. Regrettably, no standard translation of the holy scriptures sanctioned by the Zoroastrian religious authorities exists.

The Gathic tradition is reflective. It considers being, truth, and wisdom as one, and as the source. This source is exclusively good, constructive, just, loving, bounteous, and powerful. It is primordial and eternal. It is the fountain of life, the essence of intelligence and the Truth. Zoroaster saw and defined the Source only in its attributes, and called it *Ahura Mazda*. Unlike the Abrahamic religious traditions, Zoroaster physically never stood in the presence of God; God manifested himself only in Zoroaster's good mind. Also, unlike the Abrahamic religions, Zoroastrianism believed creation was not made out of nothing; creation was always with *Ahura Mazda*. In the Gathic tradition, spirituality does not have an anti-material connotation and does not require asceticism; in *The Younger Avesta*, however, spirituality acquires new dimensions and lends itself to both asceticism and esotericism.

Zoroaster propounded five moral principles that underlie man's life. The most important are man's freedom of choice and the principle of "moral dualism." While granting man freedom of choice in life, *Ahura Mazda* in his justice has defined good and nongood (or evil). He has also bestowed upon man the faculties for distinguishing between the two.

Zoroaster also preached the principle of the immortality of the soul and the concept of happiness and suffering resulting from man's thoughts, words, and deeds. He further stated that the so-called reward and punishment results from the operation of the eternal law of *Asha*–the law of creation. No mediation or subsequent repentance (except if it is followed by the performance of so many good deeds that exceed previous evil doings) can change man's lot. Man is created as *Ahura Mazda*'s coworker and friend; as such *Ahura Mazda*'s divine attributes are reflected in man and in the universe.

Morality, goodness, and constructiveness are central to Zoroastrianism. They are synonymous to holiness. Being, Good Mind (wisdom), and Truth are the triad on which creation is founded; good thought, good word, and good deed are the moral triad on which happiness in life depends.

Everything created by *Ahura Mazda* is good. Matter is not evil. The corporeal (*Astvant*) and the spiritual (*Manahya*), though distinct, are interrelated. The spirit or mind, however, affects the body and determines man's mode of life. Man as the guardian of the world is duty-bound to care for the protection of nature, the environment, and the cleanliness of the elements. The pollution of air, water, and the earth is a sin. Thus Zoroastrianism projects itself as the first environmental religion.

The *Gathas* testify to the equality of man and woman. The liberty and dignity of human beings are embedded in the *Gathas*. The only division is between the righteous (*Ashvan*) and the wicked (*Dregvant*). The righteous people will enjoy immortality and join *Ahura Mazda* in the abode of wisdom and truth. Light represents that abode; it is the symbol of divine attributes.

Zoroastrianism has influenced other religions. Dualism and the principle of reward and punishment have greatly affected the Abrahamic religions. The idea of the direct contact of man with the Source, and that which has come to be known as mysticism, has its roots in the ancient Iranian religion.

The fifth principle laid down in the *Gathas* is the final triumph of good over evil. This is the incentive for man leading an active life and engaging in an unceasing struggle against wickedness. It is the promise for the establishment of a world free of contradictions, rage, violence, injustice, and immorality. Inspired by *Ahura Mazda*'s creative spirit (*Spenta Mainyu*), sublime mind (*Vahishta Mana*), and righteousness (*Asha Vahishta*), man will develop tranquility, humbleness, selfless and holy love (*,Spenta Armaity*), self-realization (*Haurvatat*), and attain immortality (*Ameretat*) through perfection. It is then that the divine kingdom (*Khshatra*) will prevail; it is then that man stands in the presence of God–the pinnacle of spirituality.

In the Gathic tradition, creation/emanation has always been with *Ahura Mazda* and is an ongoing process independent of time and space. In his infinitude, *Ahura Mazda* fashioned finite time and space. In *Ahura Mazda*'s infinitude, no composite being exists. The infinitude is the first and the last, the finite is in the process of change, evolution, and perfection. With the complete refreshment of the world, the perfected and refined finite joins and merges in the infinitude. The concept of evil is finite and evil was not primordial. The infinitude of *Ahura Mazda* is the essence of Being, Truth, and wisdom. The evil represents a complete lack of intelligence and nonlife. Through the faculties bestowed on man by *Ahura Mazda*, man is capable of moving toward perfection and infinitude, despite his or her finite intelligence. At the attainment of perfection, man becomes immortal, timeless, and spaceless; and his or her abode will be the abode of light and intelligence.

The *Gathas* state that every good thing is designed and created by, and emerges from, the Source–nfinitude. The universe is designed and manifests itself through the augmentative and constructive spirit of *Ahura Mazda*. With the manifestation of the finite good things, the appearance of their opposite counterparts is inevitable. This marks the beginning of the appearance of nonlife, falsehood, and other counterparts of good creation. The potentiality of the creation of finites is inherent in the infinitude, and results in the *arshnotachin* or the seminal flow of creation. The dynamism of the creation comes from *Spenta Mainyu* and man's exercise of freedom of choice between the two opposite twins; it is regulated by the law of *Asha*.

The law of *Asha*–order, righteousness, justice, and progress– is the pivot of the cosmic as well as the social order. It regulates the movements of the planets, the structure of the society, and the behaviors of individuals. Deviation from *Asha* leads to disorder in society and misfortunes for individuals. In Zoroastrianism, wisdom and justice are identified with good religion; and the law of *Asha*, being *Ahura Mazda*'s law, governs both the spiritual and the secular worlds. Disorder and excesses are deviations from *Asha* and as such are evil.

In this book the impact of various socio-political forces on Zoroastrian tradition is discussed. The reincorporation in *The Younger Avesta* of some of the Indo-Iranian gods in the form of *Yazatas*–angels–is an illustration of the change caused by social forces. The concept of angel existed in the *Gathas*, if at all, in a marginal way. The concept of angels was formed in *The Younger Avesta* and subsequently influenced other religions. The transformation of "moral" into "cosmic" dualism is explained; and also it is argued that only dualism, whether moral or cosmic, can logically present theodicy.

Discussion of the rituals and liturgy, despite their importance in the current tradition, stand outside the purview of this book. Those rituals and practices represent the conscious religious response of the lay faithful to the creed; outwardly they constitute the faithful's religiosity. The prevailing rituals represent the historical evolution of the religious practices of the followers of the religion in the life history of the tradition. This book explains an ancient wisdom in its modern perspective; it may also be considered a succinct treatise on Zoroastrian philosophy. The author trusts it would be of interest to general readers and scholars alike.

INDEX

About the Author

Dr. Farhang Mehr was born in Tehran, Iran. There, under the Shah, he was president of Pahlavi University, Deputy Prime Minister, Governor for Iran in OPEC. He is a founder of the World Zoroastrian Organization, and of the Ancient Iranian Cultural Society. He was also president of Zoroastrian Anjuman in Tehran. He graduated from Tehran University in 1944. After studying at the London School of Economics and Political Science and taking his LL.M., he received his Ph.D. from University of Southampton. In 1974 he was awarded LL.D. (honoris causa) by University of Pennsylvania. He became professor of Law at the Tehran National University in 1965 and taught at several universities including Tehran, Pahlavi and Boston University. Currently , he is Professor Emeritus of International Relations at Boston University. Farhang Mehr contributed to various symposia, and has extensive writings in the fields of law, international relations and Zoroastrianism including nine books in Persian and English. He resides with his family in Newton , Massachusetts.